MIDLOTHIAN

AN ILLUSTRATED ARCHITECTURAL GUIDE

Midlothian has nothing of interest to Tourists so a former County Clerk told me. How wrong he was, and how lacking a sense of history, this architectural guide proves.

Midlothian was renowned for its picturesque valleys and experienced a tourist boom in the early 19th century before they became polluted by the paper mills and coal-mining. Now these industries have almost gone but have left behind the splendid Lady Victoria Colliery – now the Scottish Mining Museum – and its miners' village of Newtongrange – as tourist attractions in their own right.

Once again you can enjoy the picturesque charms of the valley of the North Esk and its chain of marvellous *country seats* with the progenitor of them all – Mavisbank – saved from demolition by my Trust and still awaiting restoration by Historic Scotland.

Midlothian's other outstanding features are the delightful stone villas at Eskbank and Broomieknowe built by industrialists and rich merchants escaping the smoke of Edinburgh in late Victorian days.

This guide will also help you rediscover, behind the 20th-century housing estates, the villages, churches and historic monuments that so charmed our forebears.

Frank Tindall

F P Tindall OBE MA FRTPI Hon FRIAS
Director of the Lothian Building Preservation Tru.

© Author: Jane Thomas
Series editor: Charles McKean
Series consultant: David Walker
Editorial consultant: Duncan McAra
Cover design: Dorothy Steedman, Almond Design
Index: Oula Jones

The Rutland Press
ISBN 1 873190 26 3
1st published 1995

Cover illustrations
Front: Penicuik and Pentland Hills from Uttershill (Thomas)
Inset: Stables, Penicuik House (RCAHMS)
Back: Top Dalkeith House (James Gardiner)
Bottom left Gravestone, Old Glencorse Parish Church (James Gardiner)
Bottom right Crichton Castle (James Gardiner)

Typesetting and picture scans by Almond Design, Edinburgh
Printed by Nimmos Colour Printers, Edinburgh

The *garden of Scotland* which embraces Edinburgh in a hill-ringed curve was known as *Edinburghshire* in the 19th century. Its proximity to the capital has ensured it a place at the centre of Scottish life, whether as the scene of Wars of Independence or as bearer of traffic to and from the south along ancient routes, which were certainly formed by Roman times. Shrunk during the Local Government Reorganisation of 1975 (thereby losing its connection to the port of Musselburgh whose trade once rivalled that of Leith) Midlothian still has a richly diverse architecture encompassing everything from enchanting villages to medieval churches to some of Scotland's finest country houses.

For centuries this most beautiful of commuter belts with its *constant succession of gentlemen's seats* has been home to the great and the good. Hills and rivers define its varied and romantic landscape. To the west are the dramatic peaks of the Pentlands, beloved of Robert Louis Stevenson, Sir Walter Scott and Allan Ramsay. The Moorfoots frame the wild, open pastures of the south while to the east are the rolling Lammermuirs. Sculpting the land within is a trio of winding valleys – the North Esk, South Esk and the Tyne – each garlanded with strings of villas, castles and country seats.

Rural power bases resound with history, from the brooding mass of Borthwick Castle, supreme reminder of the quality of 15th-century design, to the picturesque ruins of Rosslyn Castle. Some were adapted by Scotland's premier architects – Oxenfoord by Robert Adam, and Dalhousie by William Burn – while others were more radically rebuilt such as Arniston House and Preston Hall. Outstanding amongst these riches is the

There are the most commanding points of view, – the most interesting prospects, – the most considerable towns and villages, – the most magnificent or handsome country seats and villas – deserving the notice of the citizen or the stranger, in the environs of Edinburgh.
History of Edinburgh, 1800

Of **Old Penicuik House (Newbiggin)**, demolished in 1761, Sir John Clerk wrote: *The villa is seven or eight miles from Edinburgh. This distance is particularly pleasant to me and would be as I suppose to all men immersed in public affairs, more agreeable than a retreat nearer to the city.*
John M Gray

Above *Newbiggin.* Left *Rosslyn Castle, c.1880.* Below *Arniston House, c.1800.* Opposite *Lasswade Cottage in the 1920s*

This County has an uncommonly brilliant appearance from the great number of country seats with which it abounds, belonging to the different Noblemen or dignified and opulent gentry, whose respective palaces, castles, and villages in general, beautifully encircled with natural woods or plantations, adorn and highly embellish the face of the country.
G Robertson

Above *Queen Victoria's visit to Dalkeith House*. Right *Crichton Castle*

Right *Penicuik House.*
Below *Newbattle Abbey, c.1883*

Renaissance palace block at Crichton Castle, untouched by later occupants. Pre-eminent among the principal seats is Dalkeith House, one of the grandest early classical houses in Scotland. Penicuik House, with its unrivalled 18th-century landscape, and Newbattle Abbey, great monastic establishment transformed into secular treasure-house, are also of national importance.

As early as 1600 *more than a hundred country seats are to be found within a radius of two leagues of the town* but it was not until the early 18th century that the appeal of the villa grew apace so that Midlothian became peppered with the exquisite rural residences of Edinburgh's bankers, merchants and advocates (as well as local lairds). While affairs of state and business were conducted from Edinburgh's town houses, country villas such as Mavisbank, Auchindinny and Middleton Hall were primarily used for relaxation and entertaining. As was the case across the country, many large houses were demolished in the 1950s and 1960s, Woolmet House was perhaps the saddest loss, but new uses have been found for some of those that remained uninhabited; the District Council runs Vogrie as a country park, while others have become hotels and schools.

A host of writers from William Drummond to Robert Louis Stevenson have found inspiration in Midlothian's winding river valleys and craggy hills, its wooded ruins and ancient strongholds. A newly wed Sir Walter Scott set a trend by renting Lasswade Cottage from which to luxuriate in the stirring history associated with these picturesque delights, the backdrop for so many of Scotland's liveliest episodes and fitting stage for the tragic flight of Mary Queen of Scots. Tourism inevitably followed, much of it directed at the incomparable Rosslyn Chapel.

Rosslyn Chapel decorated for Christmas 1862

RCAHMS

Paper-making and coal-mining flourished sufficiently in the 18th century to blacken the Esk but also to enrich many of its inhabitants as they developed Edinburgh's industrial base. Rich coal deposits were mined from the 13th century by the industrious monks of Newbattle Abbey and exploited in earnest from the 18th century but other than brave Monktonhall, which was successfully reopened by a consortium of its miners in 1992, mining has stopped. Dalmore Mill is the only survivor among the myriad paper mills that once flanked the North Esk, though much of Penicuik bears witness to the patronage of its resident paper magnates. The lime industry flourished over much of Midlothian providing lime for Edinburgh's building trade and for local farmers. Though disused, limekilns still dot the landscape like dwarf forts. For a while, Midlothian protected its rich industrial heritage; mining villages such

Scott summed up the beauties of the Pentlands when describing a walk he often took from Barony House to Woodhouselee: *I think I never saw anything more beautiful than the ridge of Carnethy against a clear frosty sky, with its peaks and varied slopes. The hills glowed like purple amethysts; the sky glowed topaz and vermillion colours.*

INTRODUCTION

Of Yorkston, Monteith and Greenhall farms Robert Dundas of Arniston wrote in 1838: *What buildings existed were of the old Scotch type, not much better than Highland huts and too bad for improvement.* His new tenant at Yorkston, Thomas Laing, made such a success of enclosing his land that he left a fortune of £30,000 to the Royal Infirmary of Edinburgh.

Right *Improvement plan for Carrington Barns, 1813.*
Below *Travellers Guide map, 1814*

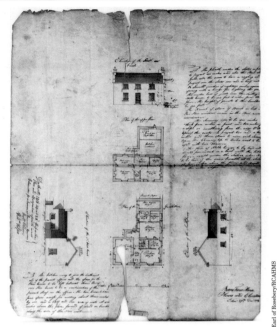

Earl of Rosebery/RCAHMS

RCAHMS

as Rosewell and Newtongrange were declared Conservation Areas, but Rosewell has since had this protection removed. Alternative solutions to demolition have succeeded for structures such as the Ironmills at Dalkeith, which have been converted into housing, and for Lady Victoria Colliery, now run as the Scottish Mining Museum.

Edinburghshire includes some of the finest agricultural land in the country which encouraged the improvement of most of its farms at the beginning of the 19th century. All the Earl of Rosebery's farms in the central belt, including Carrington Barns, were re-cast at this time. Buildings were renovated or rebuilt and thatching discouraged in favour of more permanent roofing solutions. Farming itself has changed significantly in Midlothian with an end to dairy farming and an increase in intensive cash cropping. Sheep farming continues on the southern uplands despite partially succumbing to the inevitable encroachment of forestry.

The 20th century's most tangible legacy has been the low-level swathes of local authority housing that skirt Dalkeith, Penicuik and Loanhead. Though largely uninspired these include some fine 1930s developments. However, some good commercial developments and sympathetic conservation projects of the 1990s bode well for the start of a new millennium.

Organisation of this Guide

This volume follows Midlothian's three radiating river valleys beginning with Dalkeith House and running south along the North Esk to Loanhead, Lasswade and Penicuik taking in the Pentland foothills; back to Newbattle and then along the South Esk through Newtongrange, Gorebridge and Temple ending at Gladhouse Reservoir; then the Tyne valley, beginning just north at Cousland and running south through Pathhead and Crichton, heading east at Borthwick to Fala and on to Soutra Hill and, finally, Newton parish to the north.

Text Arrangement

Entries for principal buildings follow the sequence of name (or number), address, date and architect (if known). Lesser buildings are sometimes contained within the same paragraphs. Text in the smaller columns is illustrative or anecdotal of the social, cultural or historic background to the buildings and architecture of Midlothian.

Maps

Principal locations are named on the district map: there is also a street map for Dalkeith. The reference numbers relate to the numbers in the text and not to page numbers. The maps have been prepared by Midlothian District Council.

Illustrations

The source of each illustration is noted alongside.

Access

Many buildings in this book are either open to the public or are clearly visible from public road or footpath. Many, however, are not. Readers are asked to respect occupiers' privacy.

Sponsors

The author is particularly grateful to Midlothian District Council, the Royal Commission on the Ancient and Historical Monuments of Scotland and the Landmark Trust for their generous support.

In the seventh century, Midlothian was at the centre of the *Debateable Lands* disputed by the bordering kingdoms of Dalriada, Strathclyde, Bernicia and the kingdom of the Picts. Absorbed into Northumbria with Bernicia, it was pulled back into *Scotia* in the ninth century.

Below *Steeple, Penicuik House stables.* Bottom *The Pentland Hills*

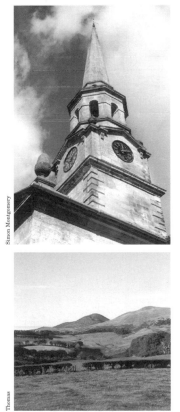

7

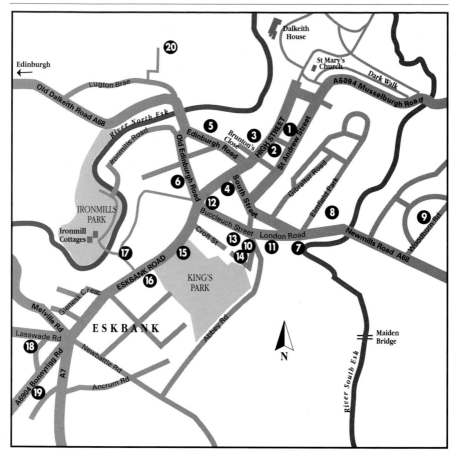

From 1919, the area to the east of High Street was completely redeveloped, the Local Authority Housing Act of 1924 having provided a spur for new building. It was Ian Lindsay's 1930s Scottish Burgh Survey, including Dalkeith, that was a key factor in the establishment of the Scottish conservation movement. The population continued to grow with the people clamouring for new dwellings in 1945 so that prefabricated dwellings were provided: Arcon Mark IV construction type with a rolled-steel framework and corrugated cement sheet facings, steel windows and external doors and corrugated asbestos sheeting roofs.

DALKEITH

Pleasant Dalkeith! With its bonny river, its gardens full of gooseberry bushes and pear-trees, its grass parks spotted with sheep, and its grand green woods (David Moir, *Mansie Wauch*). With its magnificent ducal residence and varied burgh buildings, Midlothian's county town has a palpable sense of history dating from 1540 when it became a Burgh of Regality. It grew right from the boundaries of the palace; the walls running from **Town Gates** contain blocked windows, ghosts of the 17th-century houses that once crowded up to their aristocratic neighbour. The High Street widened from here into one of Scotland's busiest market places; thriving trades included grain, wool and iron-milling, hat-making, cabinet-making, brush-making and brewing. In the 17th century, burgeoning trade incorporations heralded their status by filling

Midlothian District Council

their Gothic parish church with wooden galleries. Much of the High Street dates from the commercial boom of the mid-19th century which was aided by the opening of a railway line between Edinburgh and Dalkeith in 1831, largely for transporting coal. The grand Corn Exchange reflects this economic confidence as do the palace-fronted banks and smart new churches. The newly prosperous began to look for accommodation outwith the crowded closes of the High Street. *Few towns are more cheaply governed, or hold out greater inducements for the permanent residence of respectable families – if houses could be obtained (New Statistical Account, 1845).* The 20th century has made its mark on the town with the demolition of many of the densely populated closes and lanes which used to run between the principal streets as well as the provision of new housing and amenities. While the current road system through Dalkeith does it no favours, the success of the town's development is that housing continues to be provided within the town centre, thereby retaining its vitality.

RCAHMS

Top *Dalkeith, c.1825.* Above *North Wynd in 1937, shortly before demolition*

Dalkeith House, 1701-11, James Smith One of Scotland's premier classical houses was refashioned from one of its greatest Renaissance palaces. A 12th-century fortalice, built on an easily defendable ridge at the confluence of the North Esk and South Esk, was extended by the

It is a stock market, and the greatest market for oats in the kingdom. Carts laden with grain from the counties of Mid-Lothian, East-Lothian, Berwick, Roxburgh, Selkirk, and Peebles, arrive here on the morning of the market day. Business to a vast amount is transacted in an incredibly short space of time, and all for ready money. During the whole day the town presents the most animated appearance; the shops are full; every person is eager and busy; and the carts return home furnished with supplies for a large extent of the country.
New Statistical Account, 1845

Right *Dalkeith Palace, predecessor of the present house, as engraved by John Slezer for* Theatrum Scotiae, *1698.* Below *Dalkeith House in the 19th century*

The incumbents of Dalkeith House were always closely involved in royal affairs. The feud between the *Black* and *Red* branches of the Douglas family came to a head after the murder of the 8th Earl at Stirling Castle in 1452 at the hands of James II. Dalkeith was attacked in the ensuing battle between Douglas and Stewart supporters and the Douglas estates were finally forfeited in 1455. James Douglas of Dalkeith was created 1st Earl of Morton in 1457. The house was sufficiently grand to host the English Princess Margaret for several days on her progress from England to marry James IV at Holyrood in 1503. In 1518, when plague threatened Edinburgh, the court retreated to Dalkeith for a month. Regent Morton created a *palace* from Dalkeith Castle which was later occupied by General Monck during the interregnum. Following purchase by the Scotts of Buccleuch, the daughter of the 2nd Earl, Anne, and her husband, the Duke of Monmouth, were created Duke and Duchess of Buccleuch in 1663 though initially they lived at Moor Park in England. The house then played a less prominent role in Scottish affairs until state visits by George IV and Queen Victoria. The house continued to be occupied by the Buccleuchs until 1914 and, although still owned by the family, is now used by the University of Wisconsin as a study centre.

James Douglas, 4th Earl of Morton, was dismissed as Mary Queen of Scots' Chancellor following his part in the murder of David Rizzio but pardoned owing to his friendship with the Earl of Bothwell. He led the rebels against the Queen and accepted her surrender in 1567. As Regent to the infant James VI his firm, if financially corrupt, administration of the country resulted in a period of relative peace for Scotland. He played a leading role in attempts to unite the crowns of England and Scotland and amassed a huge fortune along the way. The adolescent king finally rebelled against him so that in 1580 he was found guilty of complicity in the murder of Lord Darnley and beheaded the following year.

Earls of Douglas into a larger tower house, then, in the 1570s, under the feared Regent Morton, into a Scottish Renaissance *palace*, known locally as the *Lion's Den*. In 1642 the palace was sold to the Earls of Buccleuch. Anne, Duchess of Buccleuch, returned from England to rebuild her old seat, *c*.1701. She had been widowed in 1685 when her treasonous husband, the Duke of Monmouth and illegitimate son of Charles II, was beheaded. She commissioned James Smith to create a fashionable new house without completely destroying the old one. As a basis for this struggle to impose classical symmetry, Smith removed the south-eastern courtyard wall to form a U-plan mansion, absorbing parts of the earlier building, particularly into the south-west corner of the house but probably into the west and north wings also. The result was one of the earliest classical façades in Scotland, dramatically composed in ascending and receding masses to emphasise the monumental tetrastyle centrepiece of giant Corinthian pilasters. The three centre bays are ashlar, designed to contrast with the render which once covered the rest of the façade. The massing is similar to William III's palace of Het Loo in the Netherlands, though Dalkeith has the grander entrance. Inside, an oak-panelled entrance saloon with painted frieze of putti, date uncertain, leads into a lavish marble stair hall which in turn leads into a suite of oak-panelled rooms running the length of the main block. These formal rooms with their marble doorcases and deep, carved cornices are among the grandest in Scotland and still extraordinarily impressive though denuded of their contents. The Duchess had come close to the throne and her home reflected this, royally fitted up in the most lavish manner with chimney-pieces by Grinling Gibbons, gilt leather hangings in the dining room and extravagantly dressed beds. Her private apartment was the most richly decorated, though on a smaller scale than the public apartments, and includes two painted mirrors of the highest quality, possibly sent from her English seat, Moor Park. The huge state dining room was on the floor above.

Above Painted mirror in the picture closet of Duchess Anne's private apartments. This little room once contained 68 pictures. Left Ground-floor dining room in 1902

Little changed, apart from restrained alterations in the 1780s which included the creation of a bow-windowed library in the east range by James Playfair, until the 4th Duke, perhaps emboldened by acting as host to George IV at Dalkeith in preference to the run-down Palace of Holyroodhouse (see *Edinburgh* in this series), considered major rebuilding in 1831. He allowed William Burn to go to town, on paper at least, in the architect's beloved Jacobean idiom but then reined him in to carry out less drastic interior alterations. He had also built a porch on the southern side of the entrance front and blocked up the front door (reinstated in 1973 by Schomberg Scott, who also carried out interior restoration work and moved some of the chimney-pieces to Bowhill (see *Borders & Berwick* in this series)). In the park the early avenues were softened by the informal plantings of the 3rd Duke who commissioned the lofty single span of the **Montagu Bridge**, 1792, from Robert Adam (but built by his brother James

Below William Burn's design for recasting Dalkeith House, 1831. Bottom Montagu Bridge, 1902

Dalkeith House conservatory with its central chimney

James Smith was a leading figure in the introduction of Italian architectural theory into Scotland. He lived near Dalkeith, having designed the exquisite Whitehill, now Newhailes, near Musselburgh, for himself in 1686 but, more importantly, he was just finishing work on Melville (see *The Kingdom of Fife* in this series) for Lord Melville who had administered the Buccleuch estates in the Duchess' absence. He had also just completed a spectacular reworking of Hamilton Palace (demolished) in Lanarkshire, for the premier Scottish peer, the Duke of Hamilton.

Top *East Park*. Above *King's Gate*

I loved its old-fashioned entrance and old-fashioned furniture . . . and its swarm of pictures of almost every description. There are several small, old-fashioned, and therefore comfortless, rooms facing the park which we were told were the quarters usually taken possession of by the present Duchess of Buccleuch.
Thomas Dibdin, *Tour of the Northern Counties of England*, 1838

after his death) to cross the North Esk in celebration of his wife's inheritance of the Montagu estates. Plain, U-plan **stables** and coach-house, 1740, William Adam, with clock and belfry added by William Burn; recent restoration work inside the stalls has revealed colourful painted decoration dating from the army's occupation during the First World War. Fabulously ornate, 12-sided **conservatory**, 1832-4, with rich strapwork panels and an under-floor condenser-heating system, designed by William Burn in collaboration with W S Gilpin, who also designed the formal parterre which once stood around it. Nearby, a grassed **amphitheatre** and the simple, classical **laundry** and **laundry bridge**, from 18th century. To the west is the grand tripartite **King's Gate**, 1848, William Burn & David Bryce, with its symmetrical pedestrian gateways and monumental urns no longer serving as the principal entrance to the estate. The **Dark Walk** gates are a good example of 18th-century wrought-ironwork. To the north, the 17th-century tower of **Newton Old Parish Church** has been used as an eye-catcher. The reduced garden front of **East Park**, 1710, William Adam, is a tantalising fragment; with its associated steading and large barn it is part of the Home Farm. In 1730, the Duke of Buccleuch used East Park (converted from the earlier Smeaton House) as his *lovely retreat*, sleeping there after eating at Dalkeith House, *greatness wearied with its rooms of state, Finds oft the secret charms of a retreat* (Boyse, 1732). Conveniently near the palace is an **icehouse**, late 18th century, with cavernous, ovoid ice-well. The **Town Gates**, 1794, James Playfair, with simple later lodge, now serve as the principal entrance and lead onto the High Street. *The grounds, including adventure playground, are open to the public*

St Mary's Church, 1843-5, William Burn & David Bryce
Built at the Town Gates as a private, episcopal chapel for the 5th Duke of Buccleuch and transferred to the congregation in 1958. Confident, Early English with cusped arches as a recurring theme. Sumptuous interior with double-hammerbeam roof, heraldic tiled floor by Minton, oak choir stalls by William Butterfield and gorgeous stained-glass windows, 1845, by Ward & Nixon of London. Though no longer attached to the pews, eight tall, brass gas mantles survive. Bryce designed

St Mary's Church

the Gothic oak case for Hamilton & Miller's wonderful, water-powered organ, 1846 (the only working example in Scotland), and supervised the whole project having to contend with a persistently leaking roof. Marble-floored memorial chapel with crypt and transept, 1890, Sir Arthur Blomfield, is well integrated into the east end (colour p.35). *Open to the public during summer weekends*

The High Street is at its widest where it begins at Town Gates of Dalkeith House. Monthly markets held here served a large part of southern Scotland. At this end it is most altered, 20th-century housing surrounding the Corn Exchange and Tolbooth, after which it continues with 19th-century commercial boom buildings and ends with a few modest houses, *c.*1800, at the junction with Buccleuch Street.

228-230 High Street, mid-18th century
Three-storey tenement its harling removed during modernisation by the Town Council in the 1930s thereby reducing the prominence of its ashlar dressings. Good scrolled skewputts. Pend entrance has later concrete lintel.

Dalkeith Park House, 177 High Street, *c.*1830, William Burn
Asymmetrical baronial, two storeys with single storey linking wing to stable and coach-house range. Home of the Duke of Buccleuch's Chamberlain who conducted Dalkeith's affairs until 1878 when it became a police burgh. Converted into flats, *c.*1965.

Militia House, 175 High Street, early 19th century?
Octagonal, rendered stair tower, once in the re-entrant angle of an L-plan house of which

The Montagu Bridge was originally more ornate. *At its first erection, two stags – the supporters of the Buccleuch arms – were placed on it, as ornaments, but they frightened the horses which passed them so much that it was found necessary to remove them. Gazetteer of Scotland, 1843*

On her drive to Dalkeith in 1842 Queen Victoria noted: *Every cottage is built of stone and so are the walls that are used as fences.*

Below *228-230 High Street.* Bottom *Militia House with Dalkeith Park House beyond*

William Gladstone addressed a meeting of over 3000 at the **Corn Exchange** during his 1879 Midlothian campaign. Following *loud and prolonged applause* he went on to the imposing, newly built **Foresters' Hall**, R Thornton Shiells (demolished), for a presentation comprising *a beautiful album, containing views of Scottish scenery, and a fine velvet table-cover, subscribed for by the factory girls of the district, and manufactured by Messrs Widnell & Co.* Gladstone's famous oratorial skills went on to win him a seat as MP for Dalkeith from 1880 to 1894.

only one oblong, rubble jamb survives. Used as officers' quarters when, *c.*1864, barracks were built at what is now **Elmfield Court**.

1 **Corn Exchange**, 200 High Street, 1853, David Cousin
Built by public subscription, this was the biggest indoor grain market in Scotland and encapsulates Dalkeith's proud mercantile past. Twin-gabled Jacobean trading hall with hood-moulded entrance and Buccleuch armorial panel with inscription above: *The earth is the Lord's and the fulness therof, thou crownest the year with thy goodness.* Bellcote and gableheads with ball finials and weathervanes. High open hall inside with double-hammerbeam roof, gallery to west with barley-twist balusters. Currently dilapidated but still in use for Saturday markets.

RCAHMS

Below *Cross Keys Hotel.* Right *Corn Exchange, c.1853*

Thomas

Cross Keys Hotel, 182 High Street, *c.*1804
Smart coaching inn with a carriage pend to right and tripartite Doric-pilastered doorpiece at centre. Cast-iron balustraded stair leads to first-floor function room which runs the length of the building with fireplaces at each end.

2 **Tolbooth**, 176-180 High Street, late 17th century
A discreet, ashlar-fronted block which was part court room, part prison and maintained through money raised from tolls on bridges over the North Esk and South Esk. The last man to be executed here was William Thomson who was hanged for highway robbery in 1827, stones in front of the building marking the site of the gibbet. Above the chunky bolection-moulded doorpiece is a handsome decorated pediment carved with the Buccleuch arms. The

Left and above *Tolbooth*

1648 date panel carved with the initials of the
2nd Earl of Buccleuch was found in the
grounds of the palace and resited here in the
late 18th century. Inside, there is a weigh-
room, which was the main room on the ground
floor, let to customs officers for use on market
day, a pit-prison (*black hole*), upper prison and,
above, the court-room with coffered ceiling. The
main front was probably refaced in the 19th
century. The building was converted and
refurbished by Armstrong & Thomas in 1966
as a hall for St Mary's Church.

Below *196-198 High Street*. Middle
212-214 High Street. Bottom *64-90
St Andrew Street*

The extensive demolition of the east end of the
High Street was quickly followed by generally
good-quality housing developments,
particularly **Nos 196-198**, *c.*1935, T Aikman
Swan, a 16-bay symmetrical tenement in
beautiful grey and pink masonry which
addresses the street with quiet confidence,
Dutch gables, swept dormers, still with its
original fenestration. Andrew Forrester's more
modest contribution, **Nos 165-169**, 1937, has
thistle-finialled dormerheads. The architect of
the modern town centre, Robert Naismith (Sir
Frank Mears & Partners), showed that he, too,
could build in a traditional style, with his
tenements at **Nos 153-155**, 1959, and **Nos 212-
214**, 1956, which fit in with the burgh
architecture of the earlier local authority
housing in the street. Recent development is
more of a departure; **Crystal Mount
Sheltered Housing**, 1982, Richard Ewing,
Rowand Anderson Partnership for Castle Rock
Housing Association, has odd, leaded oriels.

64-90 St Andrew Street, *c.*1930
The first of the town's high-quality local
authority housing schemes, this replaced some of
the homes demolished in the clearance of the
closes. Four blocks of two storeys are grouped,
those at each end are almost identical, the

The Town is spacious and well built and is the better no doubt for the neighbourhood of so many Noblemens and Gentlemens houses of such Eminence in its neighbourhood.
Daniel Defoe

central ones are emphasised with gabled dormerheads. Traditional finishes were used: the ground floors are harled, the first floors rendered.

Church of St Nicholas in the late 19th century

3 **Church of St Nicholas**, from 15th century
Known as the East Church after the construction of the West Church as overflow in 1841, this impressive burgh church retains only the ruined and badly weathered, heavily buttressed choir and a few fragments in the nave of the Late Gothic original. Created a collegiate church in 1406 it was rebuilt over the next decade, but after the Reformation the choir was seen as a *monument of idolatrie* and, *c.*1590, was partitioned off from the church. It fell into disrepair and its surface-ribbed, pointed tunnel vault collapsed. The main body of the church was largely rebuilt only to be used as a stable by Cromwell in 1650 *the Kirk being so filled with horse and guards, that neither sermon nor session could be kept therein*. Soon after it was fitted with the first of eight galleries for the Incorporations of the town such as the Hammermen whose 1665 banner is displayed on the north aisle wall. David Bryce and William Burn drastically recast the church, 1851-5, removing the tiered galleries, renewing the roof and west tower and reorienting the church from north to east. Parts of the south porch and the piers in the nave survive from the original church. The west gallery was added in 1885. Bryce's pulpit and choir rail were removed in the simplification of the interior, 1936, by T Aikman Swan. On the south-west wall is the cherub-draped **Calderwood Monument**, 1680, to William Calderwood, Minister of Dalkeith. The **Buccleuch burial vault** is in

Nave, Church of St Nicholas

the sacristy of the old church, its original lead-studded coffins just visible through the grill. In the old choir lies the **Morton Monument** with recumbent effigies of the 1st Earl of Morton, who died in 1498, and his wife Joanna. The base of the tomb was rebuilt in 1965 by volunteers who also cleared out the apse. In the churchyard, a substantial **wall monument**, 1722, to the Douglas family.

The gabled, two-storey rubble row of **Brunton's Close**, 18th century, runs at right angles to the High Street and is a vestigial reminder of Dalkeith's early street pattern. The close itself was originally an enclosed garden which was later built over as the need for housing increased. Restored by the District Council along with a façade-retention redevelopment of **Nos 107-113**. Behind St Nicholas are the remains of **Dalkeith Grammar School**, 18th century, once considered *the first in the kingdom*, now partly engulfed in a workshop. **Birchlea**, early 19th century, was the school principal's sober, classically detailed house.

Brunton's Close

Dalkeith Grammar School was originally run by the collegiate church of St Nicholas. During the 18th century it was said to have *produced some of the greatest geniuses, and brightest ornaments of the age.* They included the architect John Adam, Sir John Clerk's children, William Robertson (historian and principal of Edinburgh University) and Henry Dundas, 1st Lord Melville. In 1912 the school closed, pupils transferring to the new **King's Park School**.

128-134 & 140-142 High Street, early 19th century
Paired, bowed blocks flanking the head of **Tait Street**, *c.*1828, were the start of a Georgian development of the street that never went any further. Tripartite, Tuscan-columned, bow windows face each other at the corners.

Clydesdale Bank, 100-102 High Street, 1855
Respect is paid to its neighbours with its old-fashioned skewputts above an otherwise classical façade. The passage through to what

Above *Head of Tait Street.*
Left *Clydesdale Bank*

was designed as the manager's apartment above once had sumptuous tiled panels with frieze of entwined birds.

No 93 High Street, 1870, Peddie & Kinnear, refined baronial corner block, has corbelled turret with bowed tripartite windows; built as the Royal Bank of Scotland with the latest technology, *a great many French rolled iron beams will be used on the first and second flats for supporting the partitions above and carrying the joists.* **No 75**, early 19th century, is a slender, pedimented tenement. **No 69** has one of Dalkeith's well-preserved shop-fronts with

Top *69 High Street*. Above *47 High Street*. Right *63 High Street*

ornate brackets and anthemion decoration. At **No 63**, the award-winning Royal Bank of Scotland, 1980, R D Cameron & Gibb, with its cut-away, glazed façade contrasts with the more conventional refurbishment and extension of the Bank of Scotland at **No 47**, 1988, Percy Johnson-Marshall & Partners. The latter was, however, a flagship for the Bank's change to open-plan banking halls.

10 & 12 High Street

10 & 12 High Street, 1906, Charles Greig Originally a drapers with saloons on ground and first floors, workrooms on the attic floor. Concrete and steel structure with polished red granite facing. Tripartite shop window with iron columns, coloured glass in upper display windows and a cartouche in the parapet. Prominent flat-roofed dormers in mansard roof. Greig also built a chemist's shop at **37-39** High Street.

4 **Town Centre**, 1960-4, Robert J Naismith for Sir Frank Mears & Partners A model of mixed-use development, three blocks stand in pedestrianised courts providing an effective focus for the town with shops below

and flats and offices above. Contemporary features included the breaking up of the frontages into modules to harmonise with the townscape and the use of cross-over maisonettes in the curved section. The oblong building was built as offices for the Ministry of Works. With a significant proportion of stone to concrete, the development has weathered well. The curved sweep of canopied shops is particularly successful.

Town Centre

Ironmills, Ironmills Park, early 19th century
Glowing example of the beauty and potential of industrial buildings, with the added advantage of dramatic natural setting, a river-bounded plain with wooded cliffs behind. Iron-milling began in Dalkeith in 1648; this water-powered mill produced iron goods, including clogs for miners. The complex includes the iron mill with single-storey wing linked to the miller's house and delightful, Gothic-windowed cartshed range. It was converted first as a corn mill in the early 19th century and then for residential use in 1982 by Robert T Murnin, Building Control Officer. The harled concrete footbridge, **Memorial Bridge**, 1913, Charles Greig, commemorates the gifting of the area as a recreational park by the Duke of Buccleuch to the Town Council, 1909. Used for sports, it still has its painted, timber pavilion, c.1935.

The principal street is broad and spacious, containing a number of elegant houses, and the whole town may be considered as well built. Dalkeith is also remarkable for the number of its shops and the extent of business done in them. Favoured by its extensive markets and convenient situation, the shopkeepers of this place contend successfully with those of the neighbouring metropolis in supplying with their peculiar commodities the inhabitants of the south and western parts of the country, and they have thus contributed in no slight degree to the present comfort and respectability of the place.
Gazetteer of Scotland, 1843

5 **Dalkeith Mills**, Grannies Park, Edinburgh Road, from late 18th century
Attractive grouping of three mill buildings partially converted for commercial use. L-plan flour mill, late 18th century, three storeys and loft with an arched mill-race opening and later cartshed range. Five-bay mill building, early 19th century, with granary loft doors breaking up through the eaves. Six-bay block, early 19th century, with forestair curves to follow the line of the road.

Left *Ironmills in 1975.*
Below *Dalkeith Mills*

Watch Tower

Dalkeith Watch Tower, Old Edinburgh Road, New Burial Ground, 1827
Octagonal with castellated top, built by the Committee of Dalkeith Churchyard Association to accommodate armed watchmen during night-watch for grave-robbers.

Grave-robbing was rife at the beginning of the 19th century when some anatomists would pay for fresh corpses for dissection. *About this time there arose a great sough and surmise that some loons were playing false with the kirkyard, howking up the bodies from their damp graves and harling them away to the College* recalls the eponymous Dalkeith tailor *Mansie Wauch.*

6 **West Church**, Old Edinburgh Road, 1840, William Burn
Built to house overflow congregation from the Church of St Nicholas (see p.16) on a prominent site overlooking the road. Sharp spire, Early English Gothic revival detailing and a pulpit designed by Burn with Jacobean strapwork crown reminiscent of his conservatory for Dalkeith House. Renovated by Charles Greig, 1906, at which time the organ, designed to match the pulpit, was added. Closed in 1989 and now to be reused as

Right *West Church.* Below *William Burn's section for the West Church, 1831.* Bottom *21-25 South Street*

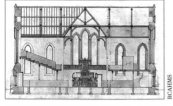

a cabinetmaker's workshop; organ, stained glass and internal wall plaques have been skilfully relocated in the Church of St Nicholas. Gabled **manse**, 1858, adjacent with decorative timber porch.

21-25 South Street, early 19th century Georgian tenement with shops. The finely droved ashlar, painted at the ground floor, is reserved for the façade, the side elevations being harled. Smart twin doorpiece with Ionic columns.

Co-operative Society Building,
Newmills Road, 1887, J W Maclean
Bold burgh architecture with a touch of Flanders,
the *People's Palace* once boasted grocery,
ironmongery and tailoring departments with
stores, workshops and homes above. Prominent
corner clock tower terminates the vista from the
High Street. The Co-op moved out in 1968.

Old Mealmarket Inn, 2-4 St Andrew Street,
c.1780
Built by the part-owner of a brewery which
once stood opposite, the irregular grouping of
buildings was reconstructed in 1874. Lean-to
porch in place of the former forestair and
arcaded cartshed range adjacent, which
operated as a smiddy in the 19th century, now
converted for commercial use.

7 **Newbattle Abbey West Lodge**,
Newmills Road, 19th century
Huge, English Gothic gateway of the first
quality. Could W E Nesfield have designed this
while he was working at the Abbey? Adjoining
lodge tower has arrowslit windows and a
corbelled parapet; the doors and gates have
decorative wrought-iron brackets. Currently
being restored as a dwelling by the National
Trust for Scotland Little Houses Scheme.

Top *Co-operative Society Building*.
Middle *Old Mealmarket Inn*.
Above *Newbattle Abbey West Lodge*

8 **Dalkeith High School**, Newmills Road,
1938-40, William Scott
Excellent period school in two phases: the first
is a two-storey, angled L-plan which, in a
rapidly growing burgh, was in five years *taxed
to its utmost capacity* so that behind is a
monumental brick addition, 1956-9, by Reid &
Forbes, three storeys on a raised basement
with an irregular plan based around an H-
shaped core. Imposing entrance and stair block
has a cantilevered canopy and windows in a
tripartite arrangement divided by stylised
ashlar columns. Brick detailing and original
metal-framed windows (colour p.33).

Dalkeith High School

Woodburn House gatepiers

9 **Woodburn House gatepiers**,
37 Woodburn Road, late 18th century
Woodburn House was demolished in 1935 and
its gatepiers resited in the housing estate that
replaced it. Square, ashlar piers with urns,
only one of the flame finials is intact. Robert
Adam produced a design for Woodburn House,
apparently unexecuted, but could these be by
him? The housing scheme fronts onto
Newmills Road (colour p.33) with a
particularly good row, though with fast-
encroaching replacement windows.

10 **2-6 Lothian Road**, 1938, T Aikman Swan
A picturesque example of Swan's 17th-century-
influenced style (he was a pupil of Sir Robert
Lorimer). Beautifully proportioned tenement
built for the Council in three rubble blocks of
differing heights which curve gently round
from Buccleuch Street to a squat, circular
entrance tower.

*Right 2-6 Lothian Road. Below 1-5
London Road*

11 **1-5 London Road**, *c.*1775
Neat terrace of which **Nos 1-3** were
merchants' houses, extended and subdivided
in the 1870s. Each has steps from the
pavement directly to its front door, No 1 and
No 2 with forestairs at the back, No 1 having
a pretty sunflower skewputt. No 3 is more
elaborate with a pediment to the street and
later Gothic paired dormers to the back.
Narrowly escaping demolition the row was
restored by Gray, Marshall & Associates,
1988, for the Lothian Building Preservation
Trust. Detached house at **No 6** seems to be by
the same builders and has a fancy
architraved doorcase with an open pediment
on consoles above as well as rope-detailed
skewputts with pedestals, presumably for
urns which are no longer there.

12 **Old Municipal Buildings**,
2-8 Buccleuch Street, 1882, James Alison
Dwarf baronial corner block extended by Charles
Greig, 1908, to accommodate the Town Council,
School Board and Parish Council. Lively
decoration includes rope-moulding around the
door and left bay window, thistle-and-crescent-
finialled dormers and wrought-iron balustraded
balcony. Municipal to the core, the burgh coat of
arms appears above the door and on the central
stained-glass stair window. There is a drinking
fountain for the public in the outside wall.

Black Bull, 45 Buccleuch Street, 1905,
Charles Greig
Weighty Arts & Crafts with half-timbering,
painted dressings, bowed oriel window over
corner porch and stained glass in big,
semicircular windows. The first floor was
originally a restaurant. Constructed by the
Dalkeith Public House Improvement Co as the
Gothenburg along with a block of housing
adjacent, the Gothenburg Buildings, also by
Greig, which was demolished in 1966.

13 **Midlothian House**, Buccleuch Street, 1991,
Reiach & Hall
Midlothian District Council's prominent
headquarters occupies a corner site. A high
glazed entrance cuts into the corner, topped with
a cubed clock, providing drama in an otherwise
low-key exterior, but once inside the design
comes alive with a stair within a rotunda
around which the spaces of the building turn.
Light suffuses the building, heightening the
drama of entering the lofty internal council
chamber, designed on a grand scale with
extensive timber finishings (colour p.35).

Top *Old Municipal Buildings.*
Above *Black Bull*

**The Temperance Society of
Gothenburg**, Sweden, influenced
thinking about alcohol at the
beginning of the 20th century. It was
felt that since people could not be
prevented from drinking it was
preferable that they do it in clean,
well-regulated premises and the
profits used for the benefit of the
community (see *West Lothian* in this
series).

Midlothian House

King's Park Primary School

Croft Street terminates with **King's Park Primary School**, 1903, Thomas Paterson, Queen Anne in cream sandstone with red ashlar dressings and an etiolated tempietto crown, built to replace the old grammar school. Quickly outgrown, a new classroom block was added, 1925, by William Scott. Nearby, **Nos 27-35** were built, *c.*1835-53, in three sections; the former tannery at the centre has wide, timber-louvered openings.

Right *Fairfield House.*
Below *Hothouse, Fairfield House*

14 **Fairfield House**, Croft Street, from early 19th century
Compact classical villa which was extended *c.*1840 with the addition, across the front, of a dining room and drawing room complete with up-to-the-minute stained-glass windows and gold-stencilled wall decoration. It was the home of the Mushet family who owned the Dalkeith Iron Foundry, on the site of King's Park Primary School. The principal excitement of what used to be **Fairfield Dairy** lies within its brick boundary wall. Contemporary with the house is a beautiful, lean-to **hothouse**, early 19th century, with decorative, cast-iron panelled base and graceful curved profile. A collection of polychrome brick outbuildings includes the original dairy shop; the tiny shed has paired stalls to one side and a business room with decorative plaster cornice to the other. Larger stable has pointed window and decorative cast-iron tops to the stalls. Even the iron water pump survives beside the little paddock.

Eskbank Road
Harrow Hotel, Nos 2-4, early 20th century
A plain, early 19th-century hotel's drastic remodelling. Primarily an Edwardian facelift (see the join at the sides and an original wing at the back) with the addition of a mock-timbered gable to the front, rejigged fenestration and black painted margins.

Harrow Hotel

*Left 1 & 7-9 Eskbank Road. Below
St John's & King's Park Church.
Bottom St David's RC Church*

No 1 has a fine, early 19th-century shop-front
and interior, the earliest and best of Dalkeith's
several good shop-fronts. Originally a
butcher's, a double curve of glass and timber
fronts an intact, now obscured, tiled interior.
Nos 7-9 a compact Venetian Renaissance
palace built for the Commercial Bank, 1911,
Sydney Mitchell & Wilson. **Nos 17-19**, 1906, is
a ruddy corner block in the Glasgow Style with
15 squat, domed tower. **St John's & King's Park
Church**, 1871, R Thornton Shiells, was built
for the United Presbyterians in Early English
Gothic. Rectangular in plan, it has a gallery on
cast-iron columns to the north and four
windows depicting the Evangelists, 1939, by
William Wilson. Marooned in the garden of
No 35 is the **Burns Fountain**, 1896, a cast-
iron confection erected in the bard's centenary
by his local fan club, moved out of the way of
the redevelopment of the town centre, c.1968.

16 **St David's RC Church**, Eskbank Road,
1853-4, Joseph Hansom
Unassuming Early English Gothic with
superbly decorated interior, 1894, the result of
Charlotte, Duchess of Buccleuch, converting to
Catholicism. Though the walls are plain, there
are gorgeously stencilled, coffered ceilings to
the chancel and Lady Chapel, 1890s, by C H
Goldie. Over the chancel arch is a mural of the
Coronation of the Virgin by Miss Gibsone.
Hansom's talents extended to the invention of
the eponymous cab.

17 **Dalkeith Water Tower**, Cemetery Road,
1879, James Leslie
One of the first acts of the Dalkeith Town
Council, founded in 1878, was to address the
shortage of clean water available to the town

and the tower was erected to hold the supply for Eskbank. Bold, industrial pagoda; octagonal, polychrome brick with ashlar dressings and slatted timber tank-housing on a stone cornice at the top. It lived through closure to find a sympathetic, if surprising, new use as a house with an award-winning conversion, 1989, Gerry Goldwyre, BBC Masterchef 1994.

Villa land then begins in earnest, most date from mid to late 19th century. **Belmont**, No 47, 1856, has a well-preserved interior and decorative porch with complex leaded-glass door. The coach-house and stable block attached have been converted into a house.

Glenesk Crescent, late 19th century, has a deep, cast-iron crest running along its graceful curve which lightens the standard villa fare below. **No 14**, **Eskbank House**, 1794, was the manse for Newbattle; a fine Georgian villa with Roman Doric doorpiece and bowed, first-floor conservatory entered from the original stair window.

Greenore, 2 Ancrum Road, 1913, Dunn & Findlay?
Skilfully handled Arts & Crafts. Asymmetrical, harled house with red sandstone ashlar dressings and a brick base course. Appealing variety of glazing from sash and case to leaded-glass casements.

Top *Dalkeith Water Tower*. Middle *Belmont*. Above *Glenesk Crescent*. Right *Greenore*

Linsandel, 12 Melville Road, 1884, Knox & Hutton
A stone firework display to rattle Eskbank's otherwise genteel façades. Towered Italianate fantasy with Greek detailing. Gunnerton stone façade punctuated by red Dumfriesshire stone mullions and balusters. Elaborate gable bargeboarding, festoons, acroteria and anthemions

were all handled with verve and the interior received the same energetic treatment with fancy chimney-pieces and plasterwork. A swansong for the practice which closed three years later.

18 **Eskbank & Dalkeith Station**, Station Road, 1847, Grainger & Miller
Tudor offices and station house with gabled wings and crenellated porch, closed in 1969 and converted into flats. Footbridge and platforms still intact.

19 **Westfield Park**, Bonnyrigg Road, 1849
Formerly the **Dalkeith Union Poorhouse**, the first in Scotland to accommodate the needy from several parishes. Two-storey, seven-bay, forbiddingly regular front, extended in 1897 to provide for the sick as well. Renovated in 1993 as offices.

Top *Linsandel*. Above *Former Eskbank & Dalkeith Station*. Left *Westfield Park*

LUGTON
Charming village beside **Dalkeith House**'s 19th-century, brick walled garden, famed for its extensive glasshouses and production of exotic fruits, now occupied by two early 1970s local
20 authority schools. **Lugton Garden House**, mid-19th century, has Tudor detailing, hood-moulded windows and octagonal chimneys. Lugton has a stretch of the beautifully constructed stone walls that define the palace policies and is tucked away above the sturdy **Lugton Bridge**, 1765, remodelled in 1816 to carry increased traffic. **Bridgend** is a picturesque row of four houses. **The Neuk**, 18th century, has a pair of sundials, 1759, set like quoins at its corner, while **Tower House**, 18th century, has a canted tower, 1853, with a resited sundial, 1745, and a curious eaves line; its bracketed cornice broken by a sharp pediment with ball finial. Three small, concrete houses, 1976, by Henry Wylie, fit well into the streetscape.

In the wall opposite the Parsonage is a memorial plaque to the architect Robert Smith (1722-77) who was born here. He emigrated to America and became a leading colonial builder based in Philadelphia.

Tower House

Greenacres, 1 Lugton Brae, *c.*1940,
John Monteith
Asymmetrical, harled house with deeply
parapeted canted window in the advanced
gable bay and steeply pitched, swept grey roof.
Built with a hint of Lorimer by Monteith for
himself. Sleek wood panelling in the principal
rooms was salvaged from the *Queen Mary*,
complete with portholes.

Old Parsonage, 19 Lugton Brae,
from early 19th century
Doubled in size, *c.*1850, to nine bays to be a
suitably grand parsonage for the Duke of
Buccleuch's new place of worship, St Mary's
Church. Smart, pilastered tripartite doorpiece
way off centre to the right and additional
wings to the back. Alarmingly luminous,
painted harl.

Hardengreen, 1796
Smart three-bay farmhouse extended, *c.*1830,
with an extra bay and advanced entrance wing
with porch. Original decorated plaster ceilings
in the earlier part and a pilastered sideboard
recess in the dining room.

Scottish Widows Computer Centre,
Dalkeith Gate, 1990, Forgan & Stewart
Vast, low-strung structure with deeply pitched,
Spanish slate roof (when constructed, the
biggest slate roof in Europe). The site was
sensitive, previously occupied by a large
Roman fort, which influenced elements of the
design; the courtyard arrangement and the use
of (semicircular, cast stone) columns. The
roofline allows maximum accommodation
within a single-storey building which sits well
in the landscape.

*From top: Lugton Garden House;
Greenacres; Old Parsonage;
Hardengreen. Below Scottish
Widows Computer Centre*

21 Melville Castle, 1786-91, James Playfair
Melville's beechy grove has long since gone
though the house is still in a lovely wooded
setting beside the North Esk, despite the
proximity of an Edinburgh ring-road bridge.
Built for Henry Dundas who was created
Viscount Melville in 1800. In order to build
his new house he had to demolish Old
Melville Castle, around which Mary Queen of
Scots had hunted, before Playfair could
provide him with a decorative Gothic fort;
reminiscent of Inveraray Castle but with an
added gravitas provided by neoclassical
elements such as the Soanian drums on the
corners of the wings. Essentially for
entertaining, the interior of the house was
planned to give maximum grandeur on a
relatively small scale. The showpiece was the
stair hall, a theatrical explosion rising
through three floors with a high-relief lion-
roundel frieze, an Ionic colonnade at the top
and a painted ceiling of gambolling putti
(colour p.36). It was placed to the side of the
entrance hall so that the bow-ended dining
room and drawing room, above, could be
entered on axis. The importance of providing
a prospect of the river for the principal rooms,
including the library, necessitated orienting
the entrance towards the slope close behind
the house. The porch with heraldic carved
decoration is a late 19th-century addition.
Run as a hotel until its closure in the late
1980s, the building has decayed so rapidly
that it is now a shell and all that remains of
its unique stair hall is the cantilevered stair
itself and a few fragments of the frieze. It has
been recently purchased with a view to
extensive redevelopment which looks as if it
will bring the castle back from the brink,

Left *Melville Castle, c.1950.* Top
Melville Castle. Middle *Stair hall,
c.1980.* Above *Stair hall ceiling*

RCAHMS

Simon Montgomery

Above *Drum on wing, Melville Castle*. Right *Stables*

Henry Dundas was a controversial figure. Son of Robert Dundas of Arniston he became Solicitor General for Scotland at 24. From 1775 to 1805 he practically ran Scotland, holding posts of Lord Advocate, Treasurer to the Navy and Keeper of the Signet and Privy Seal. Dubbed the *uncrowned king of Scotland* he manipulated the political situation to his own ends and yet his energies were directed to certain positive causes such as the restoration of the forfeited Jacobite estates. He was elevated to the peerage in 1802 and honoured after his death in 1811 with a landmark memorial, the Melville Monument in St Andrew Square (see *Edinburgh* in this series).

though at the expense of its magical setting.

U-shaped **stables** and coach-house, late 18th century, James Playfair, echo the castle's Gothic windows and have been converted into a house.

Willie's Temple, *c*.1764
A circular summerhouse (possibly also a well-head?) which, before it collapsed, had a domed roof with a pineapple finial. On the hill behind the house, it seems to have been built as a focus of a formal designed landscape around Old Melville Castle. The growing taste for less formal landscapes meant that it was surrounded by trees by the time the present house was built and is no longer visible from it. Henry Dundas was reputed to have planted specimens of every type of tree that grew wild in Britain and while Sir Walter Scott's beloved beeches have largely gone, there are still some rare specimens including several twisted chestnuts. Features include several wells and an **icehouse** on the slope to the north, a pretty, cast-iron early 19th-century footbridge to the east and four lodges. To the north is a huge **walled garden** with associated farmhouse, *c*.1800, and, by the river, **Esk cottage** and sawmill which were once part of a large, late 18th-century papermill complex.

LASSWADE
Many villas and cottages straggle along at intervals, or hang on the outskirts of Lasswade and Roslin; and are occupied chiefly as

School Green and High Street, Lasswade

Thomas

summer houses, as scenes of ruralizing, or as places of convalescence by the citizens of Edinburgh (*Gazetteer*, 1843). Lasswade tumbles down the steep slopes of the North Esk valley to the fording place from which it developed, now served by an 18th-century bridge. In 1750, paper-making began beside the river and was soon joined by flour-milling and carpet-making. By the late 1700s, the picturesque potential of the valley had been realised and a smattering of country-cottage retreats sprang up. **Broomieknowe** provided housing for workers in the paper industry, of which there is little evidence other than a converted mill building at the foot of West Mill Road. In the charming village of today it is hard to imagine that in the 1950s the village was a *spectacle of desolation* as its population migrated to new housing schemes in Bonnyrigg.

Demolition has lent a curiously open air to the centre of the village. Survivors on the diminutive **High Street** include a little, mid-19th-century bowed house at the corner of **School Green** and the **Laird and Dog Hotel**, early 19th century. Along the river to the west, the three-storey **Old Bank Building**, early 19th century, has a double-pitched roof and single bowed bay with tripartite windows.

Lasswade Parish Church, 1793; demolished 1956

Once occupied a prominent hilltop position to the south of the village. Robert Adam had designed a cruciform church for the town in 1791 but it seems likely that his brother-in-law, John Clerk of Eldin, adapted his ideas for execution. Opposite the site of the church, the hillside **graveyard** has attractive early 20th-century entrance gates flanked by square pavilions. Below is the ungainly board **school**, 1875, now flats.

Old Lasswade Churchyard, from early 13th century

Surrounded the medieval church whose west tower survived until 1866; the tower, new parish church and manse, were considered *three objects forming a group remarkable for its beauty* (*New Statistical Account*, 1845). Three disembodied burial aisles run along what was the north wall of the old church. In the middle, the tall, roofless **Eldin aisle**, created from the north transept of the old

John Clerk of Eldin, seventh son of Sir John Clerk of Penicuik, mined coal at Lasswade and built **Eldin House** nearby. He had many interests, published an influential *Discourse on Naval Tactics* in 1782, and was a skilled amateur geological topographical illustrator. He accompanied his friend James Hutton on field excursions that formed the basis of Hutton's revolutionary theory of the formation of rocks, published after his death as *Illustrations of the Huttonian Theory*, 1802. Etchings from Clerk's wonderfully evocative topographical views were published, again after his death, by the Bannatyne Club.

Below *High Street*. Bottom *Lasswade Parish Church in 1956*

Top *Drummond and Eldin aisles.*
Above *Drummond aisle*

church by John Clerk of Eldin in the 18th century. The vaulted **Drummond aisle**, *c.*1650, was built for the poet William Drummond; restored in 1892, its slabbed roof was renewed, a medieval cross from the old church resited on its gable and a bronze portrait medallion by W B Rhind, placed above the entrance. The ashlar-faced **Melville aisle**, early 19th century, houses the 1st Viscount Melville. Adjacent in the **Preston aisle**, a worn effigy of an unidentified knight, 15th century (temporarily in the **Calderwood aisle**). The **manse**, 1789, for the old parish church nearby, is a three-bay house with consoled doorpiece and stable court to the back beside which is a Runic cross **monument** to Richard Baird Smith, considered a hero of the Indian Mutiny, and his local doctor father.

Glenmore, 4 Elm Row, late 19th century, has red quoins, Dutch gable to the road, ornate doorpiece and a robust air that betrays its municipal origins as local offices for the District Council.

Pittendreich House, 1857, David Bryce Restrained baronial designed for the *hanging judge*, Lord Deas, whose security measures included metal-lined shutters and big sliding doors at the discreet entrance. The dining room has a jolly thistle cornice. Lorimer & Matthew modernised the interior, 1928, replacing the chimney-pieces for the artist Douglas Strachan who designed stained-glass window panels for the library and who may have papered both it and the *en suite* drawing room with Chinese prints, now removed. A crowstepped **doocot** lies between the entrance lodge and house. Now a nursing home.

William Drummond lived at **Hawthornden** and was a leading literary figure of the Renaissance in Scotland. Writing in English, the character of his work is summarised by the title of his volume *Poems, Amorous, Funereall, Divine, Pastoroll in Sonnets, Songs, Sextains, Madrigals*, 1616. Widely read, he amassed an impressive library of European books which he presented to Edinburgh University. Much was made of Ben Jonson's visit; the English playwright was said to have walked from London to Hawthornden to converse with his fellow writer. Son of one of James VI's ushers, Drummond was a keen royalist and was said to have died from grief at the execution of Charles I. Drummond's epitaph was taken from one of his own poems:
*Here Damon Lies, whose songs did
sometimes grace
The murmering Esk, may roses
shade the place!*

Pittendreich House

Top *Newmills Road, Dalkeith.*
Middle *Scottish Centre of
Agricultural Engineering, Bush
House.* Above *Dalkeith High School.*
Top left *Pencuik.* Left *Hall,
Penicuik House*

Staircase Ceiling at Penicuick House ⸎ Executed by John Bonnar · 1782

Midlothian District Council

James Gardiner

RCAHMS/ The Hon Francis Hepburne-Scott

Top *Council Chamber, Midlothian
House.* Above *Midfield Cottages.*
Left *St Mary's Church, Dalkeith.*
Below left *Plan, Bonnyrigg Public
Library (Orchard Centre)*

RCAHMS/RIAS

Opposite:
Top *Survey of the stair hall ceiling at
Penicuik House, 1880, by Thomas
Bonnar.* Bottom *Design for
Valleyfield Mill School, Penicuik,
1823*

35

Top *Stair hall ceiling, Melville Castle.* Middle left *Park End, Penicuik.* Above *St Kentigern's, Penicuik.* Left *John Street, Penicuik*

Lasswade Church of Scotland, Polton Road, 1830
Simple box with round-headed windows, its modesty appropriate to its United Secession origins. Jollied up on becoming United Presbyterian, 1894, with porch, bellcote, stained glass and new woodwork. Refitted again when it became the parish church, 1955. Formerly known as Strathesk Church.

Lasswade Church of Scotland

Barony House: Left *As it is today.* Below *In the late 19th century.* Bottom *In the early 20th century*

Barony House, Wadingburn Road, from 18th century, John Clerk of Eldin
Impossibly romantic *rustic hut* designed for Clerk's nephew, *c.*1781, and extended from an existing 18th-century cottage with the addition of a thatched, bowed drawing room and tree-trunk porch. The pantiled cottage inside the wonderful curved gates also dates from this time. The picturesque charms of this *cottage orné* proved irresistible to Sir Walter Scott who rented **Lasswade Cottage**, as it was then known, from the Clerks of Penicuik as his first marital home from 1798 to 1804 although the rustic nature of his *little place by the roadside with a view, a garden and one big living room* stopped at the door. Inside was standard neoclassical comfort. All this went by the way, *c.*1865, when it was converted into a dower house for the Clerks of Penicuik with incongruous baronial dormers and crowstepped gables. Extended, 1913-19, by James Tait & Co.

Clerk's design for Barony House relates to Robert Adam's picturesque cottage designs such as a *small picturesque drawing, signed by Adam and dated 1780, which is a version of a design for a hut at Dalquharran for Adam's niece, Mrs Kennedy of Dunure (similarly) Clerk's design for a hut were produced for a member of the family.* Richard Emerson, *Scottish Country Houses*, 1995

16 Kevock Road, 1958, Robert Steedman, Morris & Steedman
The Midlothian villa reinterpreted turns its back to the road and looks down the pretty glen to Mavisbank. It balances on a 15ft narrow site, stepping gingerly in two glazed storeys of white rendered brick, with a wood and glass cantilevered ground storey, out above the drop,

Top *16 Kevock Road*. Middle *14 Kevock Road*. Above *Old Lodge*

with balcony and terrace to maximise the view. The terrace is paved with lithographic stones produced by the original owner, a printer. **No 14**, 1971, is by Ian G Lindsay & Partners and has aged well; crisp white harl, steep, monopitch roof and weatherboarded gables. The tiny **Old Lodge** (to Mavisbank?), *c.*1810, has a pyramidal roof with central chimney.

Eskgrove, 3 Kevock Road, mid-19th century Imposing ashlar villa with pedimented doorcase. Refurbished in the 1920s, the entrance hall has a deep art-nouveau frieze. Superb late 19th-century conservatory with lantern apex and working ventilation mechanisms adjoins what is now the morning room. Tiny octagonal **summerhouse**, late 19th century.

Right *Eskgrove*. Below *Roselea*. Bottom *Nazareth House*

Hillhead overlooks Lasswade from the rim of its valley. **Nazareth House**, mid-19th century, is a modest baronial house, possibly on the site of Eldin House, converted for institutional use with large additions to the back, 1933, Reid & Forbes, and further extended recently. Now a convent. **Broomieknowe** has 19th-century villas of all shapes and sizes from the imposing grey ashlar **Strathmore**, its tower capped with glazed crow's-nest, to the more modest cottage, **Roselea**, whose neighbour has grown a pyramidal roof and suitably exotic lintel. At the end of the road is the original farm of **Polton**.

St Leonard Episcopal Church, Lower Broomieknowe, 1890, Hippolyte Blanc, is austere and aisleless with a timber-vaulted chancel, added in 1894, and timbered **church hall**, *c*.1910, adjacent.

BONNYRIGG
The amalgamation of three mining villages which, in 1929, merged with Lasswade. Mining was the major employer at Polton until the 1920s, along with the carpet factory.

St Leonard Episcopal Church

Sherwood Cottages, Cockpen Road, are good, late 19th-century brick miners' dwellings. The central crossroads of the village was demolished and recast in the 1960s as **Wood's Court**, which steps back from Polton Street in airy contrast to the narrow wynd of the High Street. Otherwise the village is largely 19th century surrounded by 20th-century housing; **Waverley Crescent** is an early post-war development which boasted *radiator heating from September to May*. The **Bonnyrigg Leisure Centre**, King George's Field, was developed in 1992 by Hurd Rolland from a 1960s swimming pool.

At Lasswade the climate is mild, and the air soft and agreeable. Hence vegetation is here both early and luxuriant.
New Statistical Account

The area around Lasswade was once renowned for its strawberries and oatmeal. The latter was favoured by George III and was *regularly furnished to the royal residence by a miller of the village of Lasswade.*
Imperial Gazetteer of Scotland

High Street
Primarily late 19th century, the street has been diminished with the recent demolition of Widnell & Stewart's fine **carpet factory**, 1868, which once stood at the top. State-of-the-art 1960s **Scotmid** with zigzag canopy. **Bonnyrigg Parish Church**, 1845, originally a Free Church, has an unusual octagonal tower. Ornate drinking **fountain**, 1907, in the wall outside its church hall (originally Bonnyrigg School).

Top *Carpet factory, demolished 1994.*
Above *Bonnyrigg Leisure Centre.*
Left *Scotmid*

Above and right *Orchard Centre*

Below and middle *St Mary's RC Primary School*. Bottom *Bonnyrigg Infant School*

Orchard Centre, Lothian Street, 1909, Greig Fairburn & McNiven
Built as the Public Library along with the Parish Council Offices opposite, at the entrance to the bungalows of Douglas Crescent. Arts & Crafts in red sandstone with gabled dormers, original leaded windows and corner turrets. Elaborations on the original design include a cherub pediment on the corner window. An elderly Andrew Carnegie paid for the first set of books (colour p.35).

Polton Street
Group of three well-preserved school buildings of different dates flanked by the simple, harled terrace with spindly canopies of **Moorfoot View**, 1923, James Gray for Bonnyrigg District Council. Gray also designed **St Mary's RC Primary School**, 1910, with its well-detailed, wood-panelled **hall** with classrooms leading off. Behind is the former **Bonnyrigg Public School**, 1939. **Bonnyrigg Infant School**, late 19th century, in shiny red brick with boldly decorated pediment, has become the Midlothian Teachers' Centre.

Bonnyrigg Primary School, Cockpen Road, 1974, A Ruffel (Lothian Regional Council)
Well-designed, single-storey school in yellow brick. Monopitch rooflines and an open-plan interior with quality finishes (colour p.92).

Polton House, *c.*1730, is gone but in its grounds, just off Polton Road, is a square, early 18th-century **summerhouse**, once panelled with *trompe-l'oeil* painted decoration which was removed in 1993 and reconstructed in a garden building at Stobhall, Perthshire.

De Quincey Cottage, 6 Polton Bank, early 19th century
Ashlar-fronted villa with a canopy over the entrance and unusual, diagonally set chimneys. Became famous as **Man's Bush Cottage**, from 1840 to 1859, home of Thomas de Quincey.

De Quincey Cottage

Thomas de Quincey, regular visitor to the Abbey Strand debtors' sanctuary in Edinburgh, wrote a radical autobiography in which he described his dreams: *I was buried for a thousand years in stone coffins, with mummies and sphinxes in narrow chambers at the heart of eternal pyramids, I was kissed with amorous kisses by crocodiles and laid, confounded with all unutterable slimy things, amongst reeds and Nilotic mud.* *Confessions of an English Opium Eater*, 1822

Left *Blairesk Hall*. Below *Ironwork screen on landing, Blairesk Hall*

Blairesk Hall, Polton Road, *c.*1818
Blairesk grew from a summer retreat into a principal residence. The Revd Dr Brunton, widower of Mary Brunton the popular novelist, built the plain T-plan house with a veranda running along its entrance front which has been attributed to W H Playfair. The interior was low-key Gothic but in the 1830s a more extensive Gothicising was carried out with pointed doorcases and decorated ceilings. Around 1860, a large wing was added to the east and the whole house modernised with a plethora of decorative ironwork – iron mullions, chimney-pieces, windows, balusters as well as a decorative screen on iron supports in the hall gallery.

22 **Midfield House**, from 18th century
Substantial villa rebuilt by Robert Lorimer, 1914-18, for coal magnate James Hood, following gutting by fire. Leaving the plain original entrance front, he concentrated on the south-facing garden elevations adding a canted boudoir bay and dining-room extension. An Ionic-columned loggia and fountain pool evoke warmer climes. In a niche above the loggia is a statue of Flora by Louis Deuchars, who often collaborated with Lorimer. Highest quality

Though Mary Brunton's novels *Self-Control* and *Discipline* were great commercial successes she wrote that she was more concerned *to procure admission for the religion of a sound mind and of the Bible where it cannot find access in any other form.* She died in childbirth before seeing Blairesk completed. Her husband published the story of her life with selections from her writing in 1819.

Above *Midfield House in 1985, prior to conversion.* Right *Midfield House*

woodwork by Scott Morton & Co, and Lorimer's favoured shallow relief plaster decoration within. Built-in cupboards were fitted along the bedroom corridor. Now converted into flats. Contrasting cottage **lodge** with half-timbering, 1891, J MacIntyre Henry. Exquisite predecessors to **Midfield Cottage** stood near the house in the 18th century (colour p.35).

Top *Mavisbank, c.1860.*
Above *Mavisbank*

23 **Mavisbank**, 1723-7, Sir John Clerk of Penicuik and William Adam
A complex gem, still a masterpiece, even in its ruined state. In Adam's words a *Very Small Box, and Genteel too.* The Clerks had coal-mining interests nearby and Sir John followed his father's intention to build a house here both as a summer residence and as a more convenient supervision base than Penicuik House. As Baron of the Exchequer he spent the summer working in Edinburgh and needed a *pied-à-terre* at a convenient distance. He also wanted a villa in the classical tradition in which to pursue his intellectual interests, particularly *reading the classicks.* Sir John's enthusiasm for Palladio's theories was realised by William Adam and stamped with the architect's characteristically powerful baroque style, the ultimate design

being the product of collaboration between the two strong-minded individuals and a triumph of display on a limited budget. Mavisbank sits on a wooded slope of the Esk valley. It was its setting which conveyed to Sir John's contemporaries the essence of his aspirations, *in the true Palladio taste one of the most elegant I ever saw for structure, situation, woods and water . . . you would think yourself rather in a valley near Tivoli than Edinburgh* (Roger Gale, 1739). The site appealed to Clerk for antique associations since Sir John believed a Roman fort to be on a nearby knoll.

The pavilions, linked to the main block with quadrant wings, were an afterthought when the main block proved too small and detracted from the compact original conception. The vigorous ornament on the pediment and in swags at the centre of each bay was carved by Isaac Silverstyne (a leading craftsman who had worked at Dalkeith House) and was originally painted. A splayed stair leads to the first-floor entrance with projecting doorcase. Recorded inside were a stuccoed stair by Samuel Calderwood, good cornices and decorated landscape panels by James Norie who also, as economy dictated, used paint effects to simulate marble and mahogany in the stair hall. Sir John displayed his extensive picture collection here but after his death it was moved to Penicuik House.

The **landscaped park**, developed from Sir John's father's 17th-century plantings, was given formality with three radial avenues and a canal which ran from the central axis of the house to a circular doocot, 1738. The gazebo and curved **walled garden**, 1731, lie out of sight of the house at the bottom of the present drive. Its bowed, west gate lodge is on Linden Place in Loanhead. Early 19th-century alterations included the addition of wings behind the quadrants, partly to provide a ballroom, and the resiting of the stair at the centre of the house. To the detriment of the overall design, the raised forecourt was dug down to increase light to the basement. From the late 19th century until 1951 it was used as a private hospital and known as Saughton House. The extensions were removed in 1954 by Robert Hurd and in 1973 a fire destroyed the interior of the house. Pending acquisition by the State, opinions are divided regarding Mavisbank's future. While the debate continues, the fate of one of Scotland's finest buildings hangs in the balance.

Top *Swag on front elevation*. Middle *Rear elevation*. Above *Design for Mavisbank, c.1726*

Sir John wrote a poem
The Country Seat, 1727, which encapsulates the ideas he brought to the design of Mavisbank:
A little Villa where one may Taste every minutes Blessing sweet and gay And in a soft Retirement spend the Day.
Scottish Record Office

Ramsay Colliery

Created a burgh in 1669 having grown successful with coal money. Sir John Clerk, who bought *the lands, coals and coal heughs of Loanhead* 30 years later, was the first to mine systematically. Coal finally ceased to support the town when the last two collieries shut down after the Second World War, though some of **Ramsay Colliery's** brick structures remain on **Engine Road**.

Below *Reformed Presbyterian Church*. Right *Hillwood*

Every effort was made to ensure that the church looked as if it were made of stone and since the concrete used was impure and had a pitted surface *imitation tooling cast in the concrete, by texturing the surface with a regular pattern gave a pleasing appearance to what might otherwise have revealed itself as the rough, honeycombed and mottled appearance typical of the surface of concrete at this time.*
Patricia Cusack, Concrete, Jan. 1978

LOANHEAD

Coal town with some good, 19th-century, grey stone villas along **Mayburn Terrace** and a string of larger houses along the crest of the North Esk valley. From **Braeside Road**, several larger villas make the most of the valley view including **Hillwood**, a charming jumble with overhanging eaves. At the town's crossroads once stood a **fountain**, 1902, an Edwardian cast-iron extravaganza which was part huge street lamp, part horse drinking-trough. Removed in 1932 and since lost, a pale reminder was erected in 1986.

Reformed Presbyterian Church, Fountain Place, 1875, Donald Bruce
Severe, buttressed, barely Gothic church built, for economy, with a high proportion of concrete. Since its closure the future of Loanhead's primary landmark and its town clock, added in 1899, is uncertain.

St Margaret RC Church, Clerk Street, 1878, Charles Goldie
Modest and aisleless with lancet windows and deep brick ridge tiles, the adjoining priest's house turns its plain face to the street saving its flurry of decorative gables for side and church entrance. Inside was Vatican II'd by Charles Gray and, while the east end is rather uncertain, the windows have been replaced with dazzling jelly cubes of coloured glass set in concrete in the style of Gabriel Loire. Next door, the half-hipped gabled church hall, 1891, R M Cameron, was once **St Margaret's School** and behind is another **hall**, 1924, Reginald Fairlie, its brick angularity once echoing the colliery buildings beyond, now spoilt with sloping wings in purple brick.

Library Headquarters, Clerk Street, 1964,
George Walls & Partners
The bulk of the building rises up behind, and is
entered through, a single-storey range of
subsidiary accommodation running across the
front. Asymmetrical detailing with a strong
vertical emphasis in the narrow windows to
one side of the central axis, blank façades to
the other. Built as burgh offices, it now also
houses the excellent local studies centre.

*Former hall, St Margaret RC
Church, Library Headquarters
beyond*

Linden Lodge, Linden Place,
early 18th century
Two-storey lodge with bow to the rear and
Gibbs-surround doorpiece, flanks the drive to
Mavisbank. Opposite, a small, bowed gate
lodge. Adjacent to lodge, and contemporary
with it, is the former **Mavisbank Jointure
House** which has Gibbsian bull's-eye
window.

Vatican II was begun by Pope John
XXIII in 1962. The revised liturgy
required the celebrant to face the
congregation and so new altars had
to be erected or old altars moved
forward into the body of the church.

Below *Gibsone tomb*. Left *Linden
Lodge*

On the lower slopes of the Pentlands lies **Old
Pentland Graveyard**, a tiny, windswept
burial place no longer in use. Dominated by the
blind-windowed, plain **tomb** to Sir John
Gibsone of Pentland by Thomas Hamilton,
c.1839. The church built here by the St Clairs
of Rosslyn is long gone and the parish has
amalgamated with Lasswade. Beautiful
gravestone with naturalistic floral decoration
commemorates George Brown, who died in
1765, and his sons. The rubble enclosure has a
watch-house beside its gates.

24

Robert Louis Stevenson recalled
an innkeeper's child who told him
*some curious stories of body
snatching from the lonely little
burying ground at Old Pentland and
spoke with the exaggerated horror
that I have always observed in
common people of this very excusable
misdemeanor.*
Graham Balfour, *The Life of Robert
Louis Stevenson*, 1901

Hillend Steading

Hillend Farmhouse & Steading,
from mid/late 18th century
On a busy bend of the A702, an exceptionally
well-preserved courtyard steading which was
improved with ashlar extensions and
alterations in the early 19th century and given
a plain Jacobethan farmhouse. Steading has

The Wrightshouses was a fine Scottish Renaissance U-plan villa, a 17th-century regularisation of an earlier structure, on what is now Bruntsfield Links in Edinburgh. It was demolished in 1800.

Below *Dining room, Woodhouselee, in 1804.* Right *Woodhouselee*

Old Woodhouselee, a ruin near Auchendinny, was once home to James Hamilton, loyal supporter of Queen Mary. Legend has it that Regent Murray besieged the castle, in Hamilton's absence, forcing his wife and child out into a winter's night where they died thereupon provoking Hamilton's murder of the Regent at Linlithgow. The castle was used as a quarry when the new Woodhouselee was being constructed around Fulford Tower in the late 17th century.

Patrick Fraser Tytler of Woodhouselee was an eminent Scottish historian whose seminal *History of Scotland* was published between 1828 and 1843. The difficulties he experienced researching the work made him a driving force behind the move to publish state papers. A close friend of Sir Walter Scott, he was a founding member of the Bannatyne Club whose aims were to encourage the publication of works of Scottish literature and history.
Bush House

crowstepped gables and a brick chimney-stack above the former steam-engine house which powered the threshing mill.

Woodhouselee, from late 17th century; demolished
A ruined archway folly which was built to display various fragments from demolished buildings (as at Arniston House nearby). A reminder of the richness of Scotland's Renaissance glories. Sir Walter Scott, a frequent visitor of the Tytler family at Woodhouselee, influenced the construction of the archway, displaying similar antiquarian magpie tendencies at his own home in the 1820s. The archway incorporates stones from Old Woodhouselee, including its datestone of 1657, a pair of triangular pediment initial stones from the Wrightshouses (see *Edinburgh* in this series), as well as miscellaneous unidentified fragments. The house was embellished with antiquarian features including a stained-glass roundel of 1600 (also from the Wrightshouses?) incorporated into the dining-room window. The grand, U-shaped **stables**, *c.*1843, may be by George Meikle Kemp who had added a wing to Woodhouselee. They have pedimented gables, ashlar dressings and ogee-arched windows beneath hood mouldings. Now converted to domestic use. *NB: Public access strictly forbidden except by appointment*

Woodhouselee railway viaduct, *c.*1900, and horseshoe-arched **tunnel**, 1872, were part of the Edinburgh & Penicuik Railway, later the North British Railway, and were closed in 1967. Also in the policies is the **Fraser Tytler burial ground** with a Celtic cross memorial, 1893.

²⁵ **Bush House**, *c.*1750
Substantial villa in extensive policies built for the Trotter family. The Adam office proposed

major alterations in 1791 but in fact simply reoriented the house from south to east, fitted a new stair and added a **stables** and office

RCAHMS/Midlothian District Council

court. Remodelling in 1843, in what was described optimistically as *Italian villa style*, involved the addition of a north wing which unfortunately obscured the Adam work. In 1894, Sir Robert Rowand Anderson reworked the bowed entrance bay and removed the cast-iron balcony which ran along the whole of the east front. He also extended the main block to the west and added pedimented dormers on the south front thus providing the balance lacking on the steeply roofed east front. Anderson is said to have fitted out the interior with panelling, chimney-pieces and the hall paving from **Dryden House** (subsiding and with dry rot when purchased by the Trotters in 1852), since demolished. Development as the Edinburgh Centre of Rural Economy, begun 1946, has preserved an air of parkland around this much-altered house, now in use as the Electrical Contractors Association of Scotland headquarters.

Once, 11 research institutes operated around the Bush; Reiach & Hall's blocks in the grounds which integrated well into the landscape have been left to decay. The **Institute of Terrestrial Ecology**, 1969, Morris & Steedman, has fared slightly better, still occupied but neutered with a new pitched corrugated-iron roof, 1980, Morris & Steedman. The **Scottish Centre of Agricultural Engineering**, 1962, David Harvey & Alex Scott (colour p.33), has impeccable period detail although with the wrong mosaic over the entrance because it was mixed up with the one destined for Sighthill Fire Station, Edinburgh! Regeneration as the **Edinburgh Technopole** has improved the estate's prospects.

The Bush was named after its extensive plantings. When Archibald Trotter began planting more trees in 1760, his tenants pulled up the saplings believing their shade affected their fields. A warning was duly posted: *the destroying of green wood, by cutting, peeling, burning, felling etc. and destroying of hainings was declared by James V to be £10 Scots for the first offence, £20 for the second and for the third DEATH.*
John S Abernethy, *The Bush*

Left *Bush House, c.1900*. Below *Robert Adam's proposal for Bush House, 1791*. Middle *Dryden House*. Bottom *Institute of Terrestrial Ecology, c.1969*

RCAHMS/John Trotter

RCAHMS/Midlothian District Council

Morris & Steedman

The Edinburgh Technopole is being developed into a *science city* where academia, in the form of the University of Edinburgh, collaborates with industry to combine research and training. Phase I will include an innovation centre.

Dryden Tower, 19th century
A three-storey Gothick towered eye-catcher for Dryden House, demolished 1938, with a corbelled parapet and turnpike stair. Its landscaped context, known locally as *The Pleasure,* was destroyed by the construction of Bilston Glen colliery.

Above *Dryden Tower.*
Right *Hawthornden*

The dramatic setting of the castle which once provided an effective defensive position, now, courtesy of Mrs Heinz, provides the perfect eyrie for a succession of writers in residence where *the painter, the poet the contemplative man finds here scenes suitable to their taste.* Alexander Campbell, 1802

One of the plaques at Hawthornden quotes a verse by Drummond:
*O sacred solitude, Divine retreat,
Choice of the prudent, envy of the great!
By the pure stream, or in thy waving shade
I court fair Wisdom, that celestial maid.*

26 **Hawthornden**, from 15th century
A sweet and solitary Seat and very fit and proper for the Muses. Not only is the castle in a deeply romantic setting but it was home, in the early 17th century, to the celebrated William Drummond, gentle poet and handsome cavalier. That has influenced its development ever since. From the 18th century, visitors thronged to this particularly beautiful part of the North Esk valley to walk between Rosslyn Castle and its cousin in miniature, Hawthornden.

The entrance is a passage through the 15th-century east range with its 17th-century door and original wrought-iron fittings, through a pend and into the small, triangular courtyard where the real grandeur of the setting becomes apparent. Sitting high above the winding river valley the ground drops sheer away on three sides.

The 15th-century corner tower appears ruinous but Nicholas Groves-Raines fitted a cosy library into the base, 1990. Like Rosslyn Castle, a derelict range faces later reconstruction; the north range has a plethora of plaques recording that it was rebuilt, 1638, by William Drummond, and given a new entrance in 1795. Soon after, an extra bay was added to the west (subsequently lowered by a storey but soon to be reinstated). In the mid-19th century, facilities were upgraded, servants' accommodation was created in the attic, which

Hawthornden

was given dormer windows, and a crowstepped service block with baronial stair turret was attached to the north. Building phases are clearer now that the harling has been removed from the warm, red rubble. Inside is largely 18th century, a cosy warren of small rooms. Sadly, the panelled library was stripped out in the 1970s. Restoration, begun by Simpson & Brown in the 1980s, continues (colour p.54).

The extraordinary warren of caves carved into the rock beneath the castle has prompted tales of historic deeds though no one has come up with a definitive answer as to their date and purpose, excepting the doocot cave whose boxes and fly-hole were neatly carved into the rock walls. Perhaps begun in the Bronze Age, they have been enlarged and may have been used, *c.*1340, in wartime (see Gorton House). The well here has its head in the courtyard above.

Sir Walter Scott wrote of Hawthornden:
The spot is wild, the banks are steep,
With eglantine and hawthorn
blossom'd o'er,
Lychnis, and daffodils, and hare-
bells blue;
From lofty granite crags precipitous,
The oak, with scanty footing, topples
o'er
Tossing his limbs to heaven; and
from the cleft,
Fringing the dark-brown natural
battlements,
The hazel throws his silvery
branches down;
There, starting into view, a castled
cliff,
Whose roof is lichen'd o'er, purple
and green,
O'er hangs thy wandering stream
romantic Esk,
And rears its head among the
ancient trees.

Left and below *Hawthornden in the 19th century*

ROSEWELL

Compact mining village mostly built using bricks from the local Whitehill Brickworks (fireclay being a by-product of mining activity). Built and run by the Lothian Coal Company, which owned everything except the school and the two churches, for its miners who lived in terraced rows on Victoria and Lothian Streets. Overseers lived in greater comfort in the semi-

Victoria Street

Archibald Hood, a highly successful entrepreneur, began mining at Whitehill Colliery in 1856. Living nearby at **Rosedale**, he established the model colliery village of Rosewell. He moved to Cardiff in 1867 having set up the Glamorgan Coal Co and proceeded to manage his Scottish and Welsh mines concurrently. His son continued the business and lived at **Midfield House**.

detached bungalows of **Saughree**, 1924. Until recently, the village benefited from Conservation Area protection.

St Matthew RC Church, Carnethie Street, 1925, Archibald Macpherson
Soaring individualism in yellow brick with a steeply raked front elevation and flanking doors with vestigial ogee hoods, built using local volunteer labour. The original windows have been replaced with plain glass rendering the unadorned brick interior even plainer (colour p.55). Adjoining priest's house. The extensive **cloisters**, 1935, by Reginald Fairlie manage to evoke a Mediterranean atmosphere and provide the formally landscaped setting that such a maverick building requires.

Top *St Matthew RC Church.*
Above *Cloisters*

Although by 1931 the overseers' houses were being fitted with bathrooms, the miners' accommodation was more basic: *If you go back to the village at that time, there wur no water in any of the houses. There wur only a well – there were two wells in Lothian Street, two wells in Victoria Street and a well about every three hundred yards coming up the Main Street.*
C Cruikshank, *A Sense of Place*

A cluster of communal buildings includes the **Rosewell Institute**, 1917, by James McLachlan, who achieved an imposing frontage on a small scale with a wide, concave portico which links the central hall to flanking blocks and contrasts with the emphatic vertical emphasis of their large, arched windows. Opposite, effective use of materials in the Gothic **Rosewell Parish Church**, 1871, which is in red brick with paler quoins and margins. Brick and grey drydashed church **hall**, 1932, has a half-timbered gable.

Above *Rosewell Parish Church.*
Right *Rosewell Institute*

27

St Joseph's Hospital, 1839-44, William Burn & David Bryce
Originally Whitehill, Burn was allowed to display more flamboyance here than was usual in his

St Joseph's Hospital

done at Dalkeith House given half a chance. The simple crowstepped **lodge** gives little warning of the excitement beyond. Mullioned windows give an authentically Jacobean feel and are a proper foil for the barley-twist stacks, strapwork and buckle-quoins. The lively skyline lightens the effect while confident massing holds the whole thing together. Normally Burn separated the family from the public rooms but here all is contained in the main block of the house. Projecting from the central bay is a *porte-cochère*. Inside the principal rooms remain intact, including the enormous hall with its stone chimney-piece and overmantel, and suite of reception rooms on the east side. To the back is a chapel with refectory below added, 1935, John Devlin, soon after the Sisters of Charity of St Vincent de Paul bought the house. The garden (all gone) was laid out by Alexander Roos who wrote in 1843: *had much to do at Whitehill in the way of garden with Mr Burn and Mr Ramsay. The grounds at Whitehill are not good.* **Bridge**, *c*.1830, William Burn, rusticated spandrels with armorial panels on the inner and outer sides.

Castle View, 1879, Thomas Woods
A speculative scheme, by a local builder, on the outskirts of the village. He promptly went bankrupt and sold at a knock-down price to a bank clerk who must have delighted in its confident scale. Colourful Whitehill brick with timber gables (colour p.55).

Castle View

Top and above *Gorton House*

In the cliff below Gorton House are the Caves of Gorton where Sir Alexander Ramsay of Dalhousie was said to have hidden with his troops to avoid the English army which had captured Edinburgh in 1338 (see also Hawthornden).

Below *Roslin Glen Hotel*. Bottom *Roslin Parish Church*

28 **Gorton House**, late 17th century
Built by the Prestons of Gorton, *c.*1674, this much-altered house was made L-shaped with the addition of a range (early 19th century?) which in turn was given a large bay, *c.*1860, so that the dining room and drawing room above could make best use of the uninterrupted view of Rosslyn Chapel. The entrance was probably resited in the re-entrant angle, *c.*1860. Opposite is a small, thick-walled, crowstepped domestic structure, possibly predating the house, and a rare survivor of its type in Midlothian. Both were saved from dereliction in the 1980s by Quintin Young who restored them and added a single-storey, harled extension to the smaller structure.

ROSLIN
It is still true that *A morning of leisure can scarcely be anywhere more delightfully spent than in the woods of Rosslyn* (Sir Walter Scott). Originally, the road ran in a sweep around the castle and subsequent detachment of the village has produced an odd L-plan. Nothing remains of the 15th-century village which, owing to its resident Earls, was a place of some importance. Most was built, or rebuilt, in the later 19th century. **Penicuik Road** has smart, two-storey ashlar terraces and is terminated by the **Roslin Glen Hotel**, 1868, Archibald Sutter, which was built to accommodate the stream of day-trippers from Edinburgh following in Sir Walter Scott's footsteps. Crisp touches by its engineer designer include a prominent baronial gable. Opposite, **The Original Rosslyn Hotel**, 1857, extended 1892. In an otherwise regular row on Main Street, **Violet Cottage** has been

Rosslyn Chapel

Above *Hawthornden.* Right *The Moorfoots.* Below *Empire Room, Loganbank*

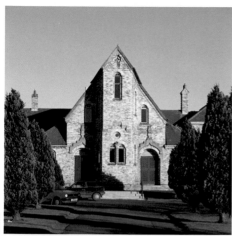

Top *St Matthew RC Church, Rosewell*.
Middle *Castle View, Rosewell*. Above *Newhall*.
Right *Empire Room, Loganbank*

John Keggie/RCAHMS

Thomas

Thomas

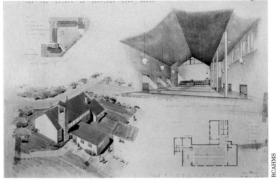

RCAHMS

Top *Lady Victoria Colliery, Newtongrange*. Above *Monkswood, Newtongrange*. Middle right *Newtongrange Parish Church*. Right *Design for Easthouses Parish Church, Alan Reiach, 1954*

idiosyncratically reworked with incised lintels and wavy droving, *c.*1950. **Roslin Parish Church**, Penicuik Road, 1880, Thornton Shiells & Thomson, was founded as a Free Church and is in straightforward rubble Gothic with a gable bellcote. Inside, iron shafts support a clerestory and gallery.

Above Eskhill. Left Rosslyn Castle, 1789

Rosslyn Castle, from 15th century
Standing above a precipitous drop down to the North Esk the castle was begun by Henry St Clair, 1st Earl of Orkney, *c.*1330, on the site of one of three local battles, all resounding defeats for the English army in 1303. The earliest work remaining is that of the 3rd Earl who is said to have lived in the palace in great style *royally served in gold and silver vessels in a most princely manner; for the Lord Dirltoune was his Master of Household, the Lord Borthwick was his cup-bearer.* The oldest part of the complex is the largely derelict, round keep, 15th century, to which was attached a building whose external wall was divided into bays by seven rounded buttresses, a design with contemporary parallels in French châteaux. The courtyard seems to have been entered through a pend (as at Hawthornden) in the demolished north range. The **east range** is all that remains of the 1597 rebuild after burning out during the *rough wooing* of Mary Queen of Scots by Henry VIII in 1544. The earlier gatehouse and bridge were probably rebuilt at this time too. Still in use, the east range is entered from the courtyard through an elaborately carved entrance dated 1622 which was added, along with other Scottish Renaissance enrichments, when the

Roslin was created a burgh by James II in 1456. Aside from its castle and chapel, what is apparent today is the product of Midlothian's 19th-century tourist boom since *one of the most frequent summer excursions of the citizens of Edinburgh is to the village of Roslin*. Roslin Glen, a beautiful wooded gorge with Rosslyn Castle at its crest and the Esk winding far below, was both a rambling place for 19th-century seekers of the picturesque and a hive of industrial activity. Dorothy Wordsworth noted: *I never passed through a more delicious dell than the Glen of Rosslyn though the water of the stream is dingy and muddy.* The Esk powered Richard Whytock's carpet factory, 1868, where Roslin's famous velvet table covers were made, a **bleachfield**, 1719, as well as Hay & Merricks' **gunpowder factory**, 1807 (remnants of which survive in **Roslin Glen Country Park**). **Eskhill**, *c.*1807, built for Hezekiah Merricks near his factory, has two narrow bows on its entrance front and single-storey, platform-roofed additions to the sides. A test case in the House of Lords, *c.*1847, established the public right of way through the Glen from Roslin to Polton, thus ensuring that you can still do this lovely walk today.

Rosslyn Castle

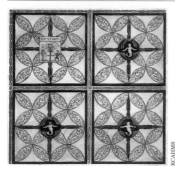

Drawing-room ceiling, Rosslyn Castle, survey by Thomas Bonnar, c.1880

A picturesque icon can also provoke exasperation: *This popular ruin . . . The melancholy melody of its tune is yet oft re-echoed from the opposite Pentland Hills. The album, the screen panel, tapestry, edges of bound books – snuff boxes – vases – cups – plates – dishes . . . everything about Edinburgh exhibits in form and colours more or less imposing Roslyn Castle.*
Thomas Dibdin

Right *Rosslyn Chapel.* Below *Gargoyle above the north entrance*

upper two floors were remodelled and reduced. What is visible above the courtyard is deceptive; there are three further floors below, all vaulted, which are built onto a shelf cut into the side of the rock. These service levels include storerooms and kitchens connected by ingenious communication shafts in the vaults. The hall was divided into two in 1690 and the southern part of the room, now open to the elements, has a carved chimney-piece monogrammed for Sir William Sinclair, 1597.

A wide scale-and-platt stair was also added around this time, joining the service floors and keeping up with the Bothwells who had just installed one at Crichton Castle. By the 18th century the building was *utterly dilapidated*. The panelled drawing room has a fine decorative plaster ceiling, 1623. Conserved, 1982-8, by Simpson & Brown, using Manpower Services Commission labour, and let as holiday accommodation for the Earl of Rosslyn through the Landmark Trust.

Rosslyn Chapel, 1446 and later
There is nothing else in Scotland to match this sculpture-encrusted, unfinished triumph of medieval stone carving which has been an object of wonder ever since it was built. Since only the choir and part of the east transept walls were built of what was to be the cruciform Collegiate Church of St Matthew, founded by William St Clair, Earl of Orkney and Caithness, its tunnel vault seems impossibly high. The exterior is doubly buttressed, the flying buttresses to the clerestory have crocketed pinnacles, and this gives the lively silhouette which has appealed to the myriad artists who have painted the castle and chapel from across the Glen. The choir has two aisles and an ambulatory at the east end which also has four subsidiary chapels, a Cistercian form probably

Masons working in the chapel, 1862

RCAHMS

influenced by the abbey at Glasgow Cathedral (see *Central Glasgow* in this series). These chapels have densely carved, ribbed vaults with pendant bosses but the aisle bays are highly unusual in that their plain tunnel vaults run at right angles to the nave, supposedly supported by heavy, decorated lintels but in reality by transverse arches above. The lavish carving of the interior has always fascinated visitors, including Wordsworth (*From what bank came these live herbs / By what hand were they sown?*) (colour p.53). Masons from Spain or Portugal were once thought to have worked here though recent research suggests that 20 of its masons came here on finishing Borthwick Castle. Though largely vegetal, there is also engagingly naïve figural carving, both secular and religious. The south-east pier, the **Prentice Pillar**, is spiralled with a leafy carved twist, possibly to emphasise a significant area within the east end, perhaps the point of entrance into the chapel from the sacristy below. A steep stair leads down to the sacristy which projects from the hillside under the chapel and feels decidedly sepulchral. **Monument** in the west end to George, Earl of Caithness, who died in 1582. In the burial vault below lie 10 Barons of Rosslyn – in their armour, as legend has it. Sir Robert Rowand Anderson discovered working diagrams, sketched onto the walls during construction. The chapel was repaired in 1739,

Rosslyn and its adjacent scenery have associations dear to the antiquary and historian, which may fairly entitle it to precedence over every other Scottish scene of the same kind, wrote Sir Walter Scott, and tourists in the 19th century agreed; for them the remains of this great Scottish Renaissance palace were the essence of what Midlothian had to offer. Staying there, they could walk the Glen, visit Hawthornden and Rosslyn Chapel and revel in the picturesque romance of it all, helped by ample doses of contemporary poetry and prose. *Of late this house is usually tenanted by a fresh occupant for the season, some meditative and sentimental inmate, perhaps, who loves to exchange the hurly burly of Edinburgh for the quiet glens and sylvan luxuries of Hawthornden.*
Thomas Dibdin

The most popular story concerning Rosslyn Chapel is that of the Prentice Pillar. It is said that an apprentice carved the elaborate column in the absence of the master mason who, on his return, was so envious of the quality of the work that he killed him on the spot. The mason and his pupil have been identified with two of the gargoyles inside the church and in the 19th century, a red chalk mark on the head of the apprentice was shown to visitors by imaginative guides.

Sir John Clerk persuaded Lord Sinclair to begin urgently needed repairs in 1739 as Roger Gale described: *The workmen have been upon it all this summer and as Sir John has the whole direction of it, in a year more it will be saved from ruin.* But by 1806 the chapel was so damp that *the pillars appear of a verdigris colour, owing to their being covered by a minute plant of rare occurence.*
Picture of Edinburgh, 1806

Top *Rosebank, former dower house, Rosslyn Castle.* Above *Rosebank Cottage.* Right *Collegehill House in 1969*

Robert Burns scratched his thanks to the landlady of Roslin Inn onto her pewter plate:
My blessings on you, sonsie wife!
I ne'er was here before;
You've gi'en us walth for horn and
knife –
Nae heart could wish for more.

Sophia Inglis Memorial, late 18th century. Primeval slab of undressed stone erected in memory of Sophia Inglis of Auchindinny by her sister.

Sophia Inglis Memorial

and by David Bryce in 1862. In 1880 an extension was added to the west by Andrew Kerr which increased the light in the nave but which is not a happy solution and one that was disapproved of from the beginning: *The western wall of the chapel is disfigured by a recently erected baptistry and organ gallery, such a method of dealing with an old building being in very bad taste (Gazetteer of Scotland)*. Has the doorway through the wall enclosing the chapel been cannibalised from Rosslyn Castle?
Open to the public; guidebook available

Collegehill House, from 1660
A suitably unspoilt curtain-raiser to Rosslyn Chapel behind, this was Roslin's inn until 1866 and as such was host to the steady stream of tourists who came to walk the Glen and revel in the romance of the chapel (the innkeeper also acting as custodian for the latter). The windows were reglazed in the 18th century and the rippled glass bears witness to famous visitors such as Johnson and Boswell, Robert Burns and the Wordsworths who all scratched their names into it. By 1843, six other hostelries had opened to cope with the visiting hoards. To the east, the stable for the inn is now the chapel custodian's office. Down **Chapel Loan** is **Rosebank Cottage**, 18th century, a quadrangular former stable block to Rosslyn's dower house. The elegant court has two-storey pavilions with arched, mullioned windows at its corners.

Auchindinny, *c.*1705
John Inglis of Lanarkshire bought land at Auchindinny in 1702 and proceeded to establish himself in a modest but up-to-the-minute house suitable for his elevation to Writer to the Signet. The house is attributed to Sir William Bruce, who had just finished work on Hopetoun House (see *West Lothian* in this series), and the

Auchindinny

easy elegance of the proportions may well be the result of his last, and smallest, commission. Symmetrically planned and originally harled with little external decoration, its appeal lies in skilful design on a small scale – the bell-cast sweep of the roof, the curve of the screen walls and the gentle slope of the ground towards the pavilions, the restrained elegance of the doorcase. Internally, the half-sunk basement is vaulted since the main entrance is at first-floor level. The rest is much altered though some original wood panelling survives. The house was extended to the back by Leadbetter, Fairley & Reid, 1914-30.

AUCHENDINNY
This delightful little village swoops down a precipitous stretch of the North Esk valley towards its busy paper mill. The spelling of the village has been changed from that of its big house, reputedly the result of a railway signage error.

Dalmore Paper Mill, from 1837
Midlothian's last remaining paper mill began operating in 1837. From the 1860s it produced paper from esparto grass and expanded rapidly. Most of the brick buildings were rebuilt in the late 19th century. The work manager's house, now the office, was in the mill complex while the Somervilles (who built the mill) lived at **Dalmore House** on the hill above. A tunnel remains from the Penicuik Railway which once ran through the complex.

Firth House, *c.*1770
Smart three-bay house with projecting pedimented ashlar centre bay and a bow to the back. Probably once rendered. Quality ashlar finishes include moulded architraves to all the windows and rusticated quoins. Oval drawing room.

[29] **Rosslynlee Hospital**, 1871, W L Moffat
Built on an E-plan as Midlothian & Peebles

Henry Mackenzie, Controller of Taxes for Scotland and author of *The Man of Feeling*, rented Auchindinny from 1795 to 1807. Mackenzie was part of the *sentimental movement*, and, in his most famous book, introduced *a man of sensibility into different scenes where his feelings might be seen in their effects, and his sentiments occasionally delivered without the stiffness of regular deduction.* Largely forgotten now, the book created a sensation and sold out within months; for Robert Burns it was *a book I prize next to the Bible.* Mackenzie was an early influence on Sir Walter Scott.

In 1866, local landowners prosecuted paper manufacturers on the North Esk for so polluting the river that it killed fish and caused people's hands to blister. Despite protestations that this was an interference with commercial enterprise, the owners of the mills were forced to introduce anti-pollution measures by treating waste before it reached the rivers.

Below *Dalmore Paper Mill*.
Bottom *Firth House*

Howgate Inn

District Asylum, the entrance reoriented, 1897-9, Sir Robert Rowand Anderson, his plain additions in red ashlar contrasting with the earlier rubble. Staff accommodation in cottage complex nearby, 1920, A Murray Hardie. A 5-ft-high ornamental iron rail originally surrounded the asylum and was considered to give an *open, cheerful aspect.*

Howgate Inn, *c*.1743
Until gutted by fire in 1994, the inn had remained largely intact, a simple, two-storey, rubble watering hole on the road to Carlisle. It was the home of the fictional *Howgate carrier.* Originally there was a brewery here too; *the strong ale enjoyed a high reputation locally and was served in elegant conical stemmed glasses.*

MILTON BRIDGE
Opposite the timber-gabled late 19th-century **Glencorse Golf Club** is the **lodge** to Loganbank, a chunky, baronial block currently suffering the attachment of a large extension. Behind is **Milton Mill**, an early 19th-century(?) corn mill which was given a facelift in the English style of the golf club nearby in the late 19th century. Nothing remains of the Fisher's Tryst, an inn frequented by Robert Louis Stevenson.

Top *View from Milton Bridge to Greenlaw after extension into a prison camp. Alexander Archer, 1836.* Above *Loganbank Lodge during extension, 1994*

Old Glencorse Parish Church, 1699
On a tree-bound hilltop, well maintained and in atmospherically ruinous repose. The 1665 church burnt down, its replacement was cruciform, transepts housing the lairds' lofts, Glencorse to the north and Woodhouselee to the south. The lofts were reached by external stairs through Scottish Renaissance doorways flanked by deeply carved heraldic panels. One of the Woodhouselee panels has been resited above

Robert Louis Stevenson wrote (21 March 1872): *My father and I walked over to Glencorse to church. A fat, ruddy farm wench showed us the way; for the church, although on the top of a hill, is so buried among the tree tops that one does not see it till one trips against the plate. It is a quaint old building and the minister, Mr Torrance, is still more quaint and striking. He is about eighty and he lamed himself last summer dancing a reel at a wedding.* The graveyard was dear to Stevenson and features in *The Body- Snatcher* and *Weir of Hermiston*.

House. The **Glencorse aisle** has a burial chamber in its vaulted under-croft. The tower with its timber steeple was added during repair work, 1811, and has been refettled recently. Surrounded by well-preserved headstones including tributes to the valued service of David Foulis and his son, gardeners at Woodhouselee for most of the 19th century.

Glencorse House, 1812
Home of John Inglis, Lord President of the Court of Session, later of Loganbank, and built on the site of a ruined predecessor. Ionic doorpiece with large fanlight with radial glazing flanked by recessed tripartite windows. Main block has corner pilasters and a slightly advanced central bay echoed by its recessed wings. Altered in 1904 by Sir Robert Rowand Anderson. The lodge incorporates one of the heraldic panels from Old Glencorse Parish Church.

Glencorse Parish Church, 1884-8,
Sir Robert Rowand Anderson
Not best oriented to the approach road but the commissioning incumbent required that his church face east, so the visitor has first to negotiate the forbidding saddleback tower which was added in 1898 and contains the vestry. With Anderson's church at Govan this was a pioneer ecclesiological arrangement for the Church of Scotland. The font was discovered in the floor of the old parish church during renovations in 1811 and may have come from the **Chapel of St Katherine**. The small gates outside were made from the wrought-iron brackets of the original oil lamps. Rock with cup-and-ring marks outside.

Top *Woodhouselee aisle*. Middle *Glencorse House*. Above *Glencorse Parish Church*

Loganbank House, *c*.1810
A thatched summer retreat for the Minister of Greyfriars, Edinburgh, which was later drastically extended by his son, John Inglis, Lord President of the Court of Session, for whom sentiment for his family home fought with ambition for something grander. Compromise was not really an option and, *c*.1860, David Bryce tacked on a massive tower with large drawing room below and billiard room at the top from which to enjoy the magnificent views. The interior is an eclectic mixture: 17th-century panelling and rococo chimney-pieces with inset painted overmantels in the old part of the house, chunky panelled dados, heavy chimney-pieces and the magnificently decorated **Empire Room** in the Bryce wing (colour pp.54,55). The triple lights that flanked the original front door have been removed with the insertion of a new entrance to the Bryce wing in the 1970s. Good **stables**, *c*.1810, extended, 1914, by James Tait.

Right *Loganbank House.*
Above *Stables*

30 **Glencorse Barracks**
This site has had a long military connection. In 1803, at the beginning of the Napoleonic Wars, **Greenlaw House**, a sizeable 17th-century laird's house, was appropriated as a holding place for prisoners of war. From 1813, building began to convert it into larger barracks. It was completed for the purpose in the 1840s and in 1875 was extended to become the army depot for south-east Scotland. Nothing now survives of Greenlaw House. Octagonal **clock tower**, early 19th century, ringed with blind windows, was originally a guard room, now used for storage. The keep, 19th century, has stylised fortifications, castellations and slit-windows, and was once the armoury and quartermaster's store. **Memorial gates**, 1934, John A McWilliam, have ogee-roofed pavilions. The barracks were demolished and rebuilt following the end of National Service.

Below *Glencorse Barracks*. Bottom *Glencorse Barracks clock tower*

Glencorse Reservoir was created between 1819 and 1824 to serve the mills on the Esk, the principal burn in the parish having been diverted for Edinburgh's ever-increasing water requirements. It drowned the ruinous Chapel of St Katherine founded by Sir William St Clair of Rosslyn who had been granted this part of the Forest of Pentland by King Robert Bruce.

House o'Muir
A large, annual sheep market was held here from at least 1658 until 1871. Basil Spence prepared plans for developing the farm cottages, though these were never carried out.

Martyrs Cross, Belwood Road, from c.1700
A small, two-storey house whose name relates to **Rullion Green** nearby. It was extended, 1748, and used from c.1800 as Glencorse parish school until converted back to a dwelling in 1859; the cross on the apex of the gable may date from this time. Recessed arches frame windows and doors, there is a circular tower in the re-entrant angle. Edinburgh architect Basil Spence rented the house in the 1930s and his children were born here.

31 **Belwood House**, from late 18th century
A charming five-bay house which was given extra capacity for entertaining with the addition of a large, bowed wing in the early 1800s. Baroness Sempill lived here in the late 1850s and it may have been she who refitted the first-floor drawing room; fine gilded pelmets (possible by Trotter of Edinburgh) remain. Ironstone stable range contrasts with the ashlar front of the house. In 1978 the original front door was reinstated and the house subdivided.

Glencorse Viaduct, 1872, Penicuik Railway; demolished
A particularly fine piece of the railway network built when the Roslin branch of the North British Railway was extended to Penicuik and had to cross the Glencorse Burn at Milton. It was unusual in Scotland in its extensive use of brick, though the proximity of the Newbattle brickworks must have been a deciding factor.

Mauricewood, from 1836
Developed, from plain beginnings, into a low-key baronial home for Dr Joseph Bell, eminent

Top *Martyrs Cross*. Middle *House o'Muir*. Above *Belwood House*

The Rullion Green monument, 1738, celebrates the 50 Covenanters killed here on 28 Nov. 1666 following the failed Pentland Rising. The Covenanters did not recognise the monarch as the head of the church and signed the Solemn League and Covenant in 1643. From 1661 to 1688 a great many lives were lost in the struggle. Spear-head railings surround the memorial from which there are panoramic views.

Glencorse Viaduct in 1981

Mauricewood

Mauricewood – as with many houses in the area – was let for the summer. A happy tenant recalled her stay in privately printed verse:
A lawn with laurels and a little lake;
A narrow strip of pine against the west;
A distance soft and south with sunny slopes
Of yellow corn, shadowed with summer woods –
These make our home scene.
Isa Craig, *Our Summer Home*, 1888

surgeon and tutor of Arthur Conan Doyle. Bell is said to have been the inspiration for Sherlock Holmes' deductive skills. South bay with double drawing room and tower added in 1859. Bell added the north wing, dormer pediment dated 1897, to provide a study and nurseries for his grandchildren. Internal improvements of this date include panelled dining room with fitted butler's pantry adjacent, complete with baize-lined cupboards. A curling pond to the front has been grassed over.

Below *Marchwell*. Middle *Aaron Nursing Home*. Bottom *Nursery mural, Beeslack*

32 **Marchwell**, 1965, Morris & Steedman
Single-storey house designed around a circle to recall the shielings of the Pentlands beneath which it shelters. The curve of the house is continued with a low boundary wall which completes the ring in a protective sweep.

Aaron Nursing Home (Beeslack),
Edinburgh Road, 1855-7, J A Bell
Castellated home of Sir John Cowan whose father, the paper baron of Penicuik, had employed Bell at Valleyfield Mill to provide a school. Beeslack is in pared-down Gothic. Bell designed stained-glass windows to the hall and staircase. Windows of the principal rooms have bronze sashes. The first-floor nursery was painted with biblical scenes from the life of Joseph by Julius Miller. Even the basement cellar walls were decorated and Bacchus was painted raising his cup to the wine store. James Tait added a staff extension to the rear, *c.*1900. Gladstone stayed here during his 1890 election campaign in Midlothian. **Beeslack High School**, 1984, Peter Williams for Lothian Regional Council, is out of sight of the house, beside the **lodge**, in uncompromising red brick.

RCAHMS

33 Penicuik House, 1761-78, Sir James Clerk & John Baxter

Palladianism took root in Scotland with this house and there is nothing else in the country quite like it. Though a ruin, gutted by fire in 1899, its fine Ionic portico and clean, symmetrical lines are still evident. Although its plan was less radical than its exterior, time has eradicated that distraction from the finely crafted shell. With his sympathetically designed pavilion wings of 1857, David Bryce proved that a master of the baronial could also handle classicism. The rear elevation has unexpected features such as the later, heavy pediments over the dining-room windows, Venetian windows which once terminated the façade, now superseded by the plainer-windowed wings and, in place of a central pediment, a trio of arched windows which lit the library. The entrance hall was *adorned with statuary and with Roman antiquities from Cramond and Middlebie* and its drawing-room ceiling was decorated by Alexander Runciman with scenes from the story of Ossian. The stair hall also had a fine painted ceiling (colour pp.33,34).

Penicuik House and stables

Sir John Clerk of Penicuik described his pleasure grounds: *I have various fish ponds, and one especially which forms a lake rather than a pond. It supports a great multitude of fish which, either from natural joy or with the desire of catching flies, are seen continually to skip and play and throw themselves about. Here, therefore, for walking, or fishing, or hunting, my whole family at times take exercise.*
John M Gray

Penicuik House in the 18th century

RCAHMS

Sir John Clerk's poem *The Country Seat*, 1727, begins

*Would you, my Friend avoid the
noisy Town
And from the Cares and Toils of Life
be free?
Would you unbend your thoughts,
and thus acquire
Fresh Oyl to lighten up the vital
Flame?
Choose then a rural Life in Such a
Field
As EDEN'S Garden best resemble
can
Where first th'Almighty Power
established Man.*

Ossian *was a third-century Gaelic warrior poet* and the subject of an 18th-century *cause célèbre* in Scotland when James MacPherson *translated* a cycle of what he claimed were authentic Ossianic verses. The works were embraced by the Scots and hailed as proof of a national tradition of verse to match the classics of Greece and Rome. His fraudulent recasting of the tales had an enormous impact within Europe as the Romantic movement began and they played a part in the 19th-century fascination with the Highlands.

Right Penicuik House and stables. *Below* Knight's Law Tower. *Bottom* Arthur's O'on

The stables and offices are superb. A courtyard of two storeys with an ashlar entrance façade and high clock steeple finished in 1766, it was converted to the family home by James Tait, finished by Lessels & Taylor in 1902. Doorcases and chimney-pieces salvaged from the old house have been cleverly incorporated into the new and the courtyard turned into a delightful garden. On the range facing the steeple is the doocot, a domed replica of the (probably Roman) building near Falkirk known as Arthur's O'on whose destruction in 1743 was lamented by antiquarians such as Sir James. The transformation of courtyard continues, Law & Dunbar-Nasmith adapting a further range in 1993. Penicuik House lies within one of Scotland's greatest landscaped parks, laid out from 1700 by Sir John Clerk around Old Penicuik House (Newbiggin) as a realisation of the pastoral ideals he expressed in his poem *The Country Seat* and subsequently rendered less formal when the new house was built by his son. Architectural features are used to terminate vistas: to the north, the round, castellated **Knight's Law Tower**, 1750, designed by Sir John to serve as a doocot as well as eye-catcher; on the ridge to the south-east, an **obelisk** memorial to Allan Ramsay,

1759, reached by the **Centurion's Bridge**, 1738. Nearby are the remains of **Ravensneuk Castle**.

Incorporated into the crescent-shaped old walled garden is a two-storey, brick gazebo, **Eskfield**, an exquisite doll's house, *c.*1730, with urns on its open pediment and a room decorated with a sculpted frieze of classical scenes, for visiting proprietors rather than its resident gardener. On an axis within the crescent was a witches' coven of stone slabs. Another **walled garden**, 1870, lies to the north-west. The *frightful cave* of Hurley Cove, 1741-3, Sir John Clerk, is a tunnel which runs through to the secluded Hurley Pond. The **Chinese Bridge** and **Chinese Gates**, 1758, James Blaikie (the master carpenter of Penicuik House), are currently being restored. **Spear Lodge**, 1872-3, Peddie & Kinnear, has a sculpted panel illustrating the motto of the Clerk family *Free for a Blast* (they won the estate of Penicuik in a hunting wager with King Robert Bruce).

The house stands as the leading exemplar of Palladian ideals in Scotland and the Penicuik House Preservation Trust is hoping to keep it as such. *Grounds open to the public once a year under Scotland's Gardens Scheme, or by written appointment*

Ramsay Memorial

Ravensneuk Castle was used as a quarry by Sir John's father, much to his son's indignation: *it was against my inclination that it was pulled down, if I had stones in readiness I would repair it. Old houses and towers are, I think, the Honour and Pride of a Country.*

Above *Spear Lodge*. Left *Brunstane Castle*. Below *Eskfield*

34 **Brunstane Castle**, 16th century
Ruins of a substantial courtyard house with interesting detailing; ashlar dressings, datestone with the Crichton arms, 1568, fireplaces, oval gunloops and a tower to the north. The house was burnt after the laird was discovered to be associated with the Protestant reformist, George Wishart, who was executed by Cardinal Beaton.

In 1836, Penicuik *produced daily a quantity of paper 20 miles long. Upwards of £24,000 per annum is derived by the Government from this beautiful manufacture in the shape of duty, which amounts to about 30 per cent. This is supposed to equal the whole amount paid by Ireland to the revenue on this article.*
New Statistical Account, 1845

In former times there appears from the remains of towers and mansions scattered up and down, to have been many proprietors of consequence in the parish, whose history is now lost.
Statistical Account, 1793

Messrs Alexander Cowan & Sons are among the oldest, best known and most extensive manufacturers of paper in Scotland. They have three mills at Penicuik; but as these stand within a few hundred yards of each other, they are worked as one establishment.
Groome's Gazetteer

Scotmid, High Street

PENICUIK

Against a spectacular Pentland backdrop, the town laid out by Sir James Clerk of Penicuik, c.1770, *has a well-built airy appearance, superior to that of most towns of its size.* Unlike Dalkeith, it would be possible to visit the town without realising that a great estate lay a stone's throw away. Initially a mining town, Penicuik grew rich with paper-making, its prosperity evident by 1793: *tea, that very expensive article, is frequently drunk even amongst the lowest of people.* By 1836, *the manufacturing population are in the receipt of regular and good wages, their houses present on the whole a greater appearance of comfort than is generally to be met with in the cottages of our peasantry (New Statistical Account).* During

the 19th century, the mill-owning Cowan family became a major influence on town life, erecting buildings and participating in everything from politics and religion to the founding of a local library. Penicuik has swollen enormously during the 20th century with acres of housing schemes of varying quality, some put up for incoming miners, putting pressure on the town's old core.

The town centre has a dual identity; the High Street runs down from the parish church, following its 18th-century line, and politely ignores the 20th century with its largely 19th-century commercial frontages (excepting the **Old Crown Inn**, 1754). John Street leads off it and is, by contrast, a thoroughly modern redevelopment, pedestrianised and uncompromising. To the north are the 20th-century housing schemes, to the south, Penicuik House and the older suburbs (colour p.33).

There is a neat, small inn about the middle of the old town, which was a good deal frequented by parties of pleasure from Edinburgh in summer to see the House of Pennycuik (sic) and its fine paintings, particularly Ossian's Hall, and the pleasure ground around the house.
Statistical Account, 1793

High Street

The northern side steps back on a terrace above the road. **Scotmid** has a fine, bowed shop-front with balustraded parapet, 1905, a speedy, post fire-damage rebuild by Kinross & Tarbolton using local builder James Tait. Once the *store* of the Penicuik Co-operative Association which also ran the now derelict bakehouse and Co-op dairy, 1875, behind, a little brick group huddling from proposed demolition. Another Cowan commission for J A Bell was the amphora-crowned **well**, 1864; part of the family's improvement of the town's access to water supply.

High Street, c.1910

St Mungo's, Penicuik Parish Church,
High Street, 1771

Sturdy box attributed to Sir James Clerk of Penicuik, its monumental Doric portico dominates the façade and leads straight onto the street. The clock, which interrupts the elegant severity of the pediment, is an addition of 1840. In 1837 it was extended to seat an extra 300 worshippers, since the cotton mill had greatly increased the population of Penicuik, and heating was installed to keep them there. Refitted internally yet again and extended in 1880, the orientation of the interior was reversed to fit the organ. Airy, plain interior with 1960s stained-glass lights. Adjacent is a **hearse house**, 1800.

The first mention of Hiring Fairs in Penicuik is in the almanac of 1802. Then, as now; they were held on the third Friday of March and the first Friday of October. Within the recollection of middle-aged inhabitants, the gatherings of farmers and their servants on the village streets upon these occasions were very great. Confectionery stands and travelling shops filled the space from the church to the well and visitors from all directions added to the throng.
Annals of Penicuik

Rab and his Friends was an extraordinarily popular tale written by Dr John Brown in 1859. The Jacksons were the inspiration for the principal family – the Nobles, a Howgate carrier and his wife, in a tale woven with that of the dog, Rab. The memorial plaque has a bronze profile portrait of a dog.

Left *St Mungo's*. Below *35 High Street*

In the graveyard behind are the remains of the old church, **St Kentigern's**, 17th century (colour p.36). The tower, repaired 1733-40 at the expense of Sir John Clerk, remains intact against the west wall and still serves as the belfry. Used as a lock-up in the 1830s. It bears a plaque commemorating the Jacksons who were celebrated in *Rab and his Friends*. Burial enclosures fill the space once occupied by the

church. **No 35** (former manse), High Street, *c.*1805, has adopted the pavilion-blocked wings of the demolished original manse.

Right *Clerk of Penicuik Mausoleum.* Below *Council Offices*

The Institute comprises a hall *capable of holding 700 people, with side-rooms, a reference and circulating library, reading-rooms, museum, gymnasium and baths. A profitable hour may here be spent by the visitor at a nominal charge.* Handy Guide to Penicuik, *1911*

Below *15 John Street.* Bottom *Salvation Army Hall*

Mausoleum, 1684, Sir John Clerk
Chunky family sepulchre in the form of a vaulted, pyramid-roofed cube, its broken, cherubim-ringed urn-finial lies beside.

Council Offices (formerly **Cowan Institute**), High Street, 1893, Campbell Douglas & Morrison
A stolid, red municipal exercise in Scottish baronial with a tall, ogee-roofed tower and rampant thistles which competes with St Mungo's to dominate the street. The Cowans had hoped that their friend F T Pilkington would build their biggest addition to the Penicuik townscape but he was too ill. The projecting clock on spindly brackets, which was added by the Cowans in 1901, is a copy of the Canongate Tolbooth clock (see *Edinburgh* in this series) which was opposite their city residence. The interior was adapted, 1963, by R J Naismith, and the council room is a stylish period piece. Still used as the community's function rooms but now also houses Midlothian District County Court.

John Street
Pedestrianised and developed with small blocks of shops in the 1980s, by the Comprehensive Design Group. An original,

early 19th-century, detached house at **No 15** and, defiantly red brick in a sea of yellow, the **Salvation Army Hall**, 1935. **Nos 41-47**, mid-19th century, have lovely original lozenge glazing. Beyond the row of mid-19th-century villas, housing by R J Naismith, Sir Frank Mears & Partners, which includes a row of shops with corner clock tower, 1953 (colour p.36). The earliest of this swathe of 20th-century housing is the sub Garden City swept gabled rows from Pentland Terrace to **Carlops Avenue**, 1927-39, by T Bowhill Gibson. Later decades produced progressively plainer homes to increasingly nondescript layouts.

At the corner of West Street is the diminutive baronial **District Council Chambers**, 1916. The **South Church Halls**, *c.*1843, are an austere contrast in economical Gothic and originally built as the first Penicuik Free Church, becoming the church hall after 1862. The road runs into **Bog Road** and progresses from villas to bungalows.

No 24, 1896, in John Kinross' effortless pared baronial, was originally the manse for the Free Church. **No 37** is a perfectly preserved 1930s bungalow.

St James the Less Episcopal Church, Broomhill Road, 1882, R T N Speir
From 1887 to 1889, H O Tarbolton worked with John Kinross, who had worked on the original building, to create a more imposing mass by adding a larger chancel with vestry below.

From top: *41-47 John Street; District Council Chambers; Carlops Avenue; South Church Halls; 37 Bog Road.* Left *24 Bog Road*

St James the Less Episcopal Church

Deborah Mays

The stark lines of the crenellated tower are relieved by finely carved animal stops to the lancet hood mouldings. Internal enrichment included the oak altar rails and rood screen, designed by Tarbolton and carved by Scott Morton & Company, 1911-12. The painted panelled **reredos**, 1921, by Meredith-Williams, is a war memorial and has been relocated to accommodate the altar. Beautiful stained glass in the chancel by Charles E Kempe. The quality of finish in the church is carried through to the new **church hall**, 1978, Eric Stevenson.

In the 1890s, James Cossar Ewart, Professor of Natural History, carried out the *Penicuik Experiment* into hereditary traits with his herd of hybrid zebras in the grounds of Craigiebield.

Thomas

Navaar House Hotel, Bog Road
A white-harled, half-timbered, red-roofed and tile-hung surprise amidst a sea of stone villas. Gables decorated with cherub roundels. Originally built as The Bungalow and extended upwards *c.*1910.

Right *Navaar House Hotel*.
Below *Craigiebield House Hotel*

Thomas

Craigiebield House Hotel, 1883-5, George Washington Browne
Villa which reflects the profession of its zoologist owner. The animals carved on the timber corbels of the bay window overlooking the garden were just part of the carved decoration planned, but never completed; note the prepared blocks over the Gothic door and windows. Used as Municipal Buildings from 1948 to 1963.

Thomas

Penicuik School

Penicuik School, Carlops Road, 1935-7, William Scott
A very good example of its type, its façade is an essay in refinement with an ashlar first floor, rendered above with rusticated, projecting entrance bays. Extensive original ironwork on the low boundary wall whose corner piers have shallow, recessed panels.

The Square is attractively grouped beside a small green; begun in the late 18th century it has been progressively aggrandised with an early 19th-century town house with pilastered shop-front at **No 24** and a strange pair at **No 18**, 1860, with corbelled oriels. Opposite is a converted **corn mill**, 1811.

Park End, 22-34 Bridge Street, 1860, F T Pilkington
Designed around a courtyard to house single women working for Charles Cowan at Valleyfield Mill. Titled on the cusped arch over the pend. As usual Pilkington emphasised the vertical elements; Romanesque windows project into hipped gables and huge chimneys dominate the roofline. A little decoration goes a long way, lusciously crisp, carved stonework detailing contrasts with the rock-faced masonry (colour p.36).

Top *The Square*. Above *Park End*

25 Croft Street, 1897
Built as the rectory for St James the Less, by John Kinross or H O Tarbolton, rather severe with low-key detailing; the first-floor chapel is lit with cusped windows, the blank entrance gable has a diffident decorated panel with bishop's mitre. The service block has a deep, swept roof with gabled vents.

Above *25 Croft Street*.
Left *Valleyfield Mills at the turn of the century*

Valleyfield Mills (demolished in 1975) was Midlothian's premier paper mill. Founded in 1709, it was one of three run at Penicuik by the Cowan family from 1779 until 1966, with an interim closure for the Napoleonic Wars.

French Prisoners' Monument, 1830, Thomas Hamilton
A Greek tomb in immaculate ashlar on the slope overlooking the site of Valleyfield Mills, the monument bears a moving tribute from the *inhabitants of this Parish desiring to remember*

By 1810, the Napoleonic Wars had so disrupted trade, the Cowans sold Valleyfield Paper Mill to the government to use as one of three holding places in the area for prisoners of war. Robert Reid as government architect adapted the mill and *a complete change took place on the premises, by the erection of new buildings, dismantling and changing the appropriation of others, and converting the whole space of ground into prison yards, which were partly paved and partly covered with gravel, forming on the whole an extensive and suitable depot for the accommodation of upwards of five thousand prisoners, with barracks and guard houses for the troops on duty. The premises continued to be thus occupied until the conclusion of the War in 1814.* Ian MacDougall, *The Prisoners at Penicuik*, 1989

that all men are bretheren to the 309 who failed to survive incarceration. It was largely paid for by the Cowan family.

Valleyfield Mill School, 1823, J A Bell
Built for the mill workers in simple, picturesque, Tudor Gothic with single-storey blocks set at right angles and linked by a gabled porch and Gothic bellcote. At its height, over 100 children attended daily. In 1890 it became a canteen. Now converted for residential use (colour p.34).

Valleyfield House, *c.*1810, Robert Reid
Keeping a watchful eye on the prison camp from the hill above, the house was divided in two for its governor and, possibly, chaplain. Massive blocks of stone channelled to seem more refined on the original two storeys. Bought by the Cowans after the Napoleonic Wars and extended with a billiard room. Porch, *c.*1830, Thomas Hamilton?

Top *French Prisoners' Monument.*
Middle *Valleyfield Mill School before the demolition of the mill.* Above *Valleyfield House.* Right *Penicuik South Church*

Penicuik South Church, Bridge Street,
1862, F T Pilkington
Extraordinarily striking structure. Originally
built as Penicuik Free Church replacing the
first church (see West Street).
Characteristically, the maverick architect used
dramatic contrasts of scale; the weighty
entrance is supported on tiny shafts and there
was to have been a tall, dominant spire on the
existing squat tower. Heavily floriated capitals
decorate the explosion of geometry, while inside
the complex form of the varnished wooden
ceiling dominates the space. The plan is a
square set diagonally to the main axis with its
corners removed, apart from the east corner
which extends into a galleried area. Shafts
beside the pulpit are decorated with small
polished bosses.

Penicuik South Church

Uttershill Castle, Pomathorn Road,
from *c.*1510
An excellent viewing point from which to
appreciate Penicuik's Pentland setting. The
original house consisted of the vaulted western
block which was later extended with a linking
transverse corridor to a kitchen wing. An extra
storey was added with elegantly large windows
from which to survey more peaceful times,
possibly *c.*1646, when it was the home of the
Countess of Eglinton. Ruined since the early
19th century there are plans to restore it as a
house.

YMCA (former **Kirkhill School**),
Kirkhill Road, 1859, F T Pilkington
Kirkhill itself was built to house spinners from
Scotland's first cotton mill, Esk Mill, 1778, and
commands extensive views over the county from
the same height as Arthur's Seat in Edinburgh.
Though Pilkington added only a small
extension to the 1845-6 Free Church school, it
was his first collaboration with the Cowan
family of Penicuik, the result of his Edinburgh
University friendship with John Cowan. It gives
little hint of the flamboyance he brought to
subsequent projects. Penicuik was once richer
in Pilkingtonia; his largest project, **Woodslee
House**, was demolished in 1967.

Top *Uttershill Castle during
excavation, 1994*. Above *YMCA*

Woodslee House in 1865

SILVERBURN
Right at the foot of the Pentlands, a little
settlement which grew up around the sawmill
of the Penicuik House estate, now **Silverburn
Farm**. **Carnethy**, 1803, was individualised

with lively carved decoration, 1855, to the front and rear. Over the back door is a profile portrait of Queen Victoria. The cottage was sympathetically extended in 1993. Down the hill are two houses by Leslie Grahame Thomson: a Spanish bungalow, **Look About Ye**, 1939, and a larger, similarly white-harled house of 1954, both with uninterrupted views of the Moorfoots (colour p.54).

35 **Bavelaw Castle**, early 17th century
Over the other side of the Pentlands to the west, an L-plan laird's house with crowstepped gables and a round tower at the north-east angle. The hall has an ornamental plaster ceiling and was pine panelled, *c.*1783, when it was acquired by Johnston Merchants of Gothenburg, the centre of the quality pine trade in the 18th century. Altered by Sir Robert Lorimer. (Now within the district of Edinburgh.)

Ninemileburn
Little settlement around the old **Habbie's Howe Inn**, named after the *Gentle Shepherd* associated with Newhall. The late 18th-century, rendered inn once had a quotation from the poem over its porch but is now closed and the panel painted over. Single-storey rubble wing to the side.

From top: *Carnethy*; *Detail of former doorway, Carnethy*; *Bavelaw Castle*; *Habbie's Howe Inn, c.1910.* Right *Look About Ye*

36 **Newhall**, 1704 onwards
A recasting of an earlier house forms the core of Newhall. Two 1704 rooms survive intact: the panelled advocate's room and library. In the late 18th century, Robert Brown embellished the landscape around his home to celebrate its role as an inspiration for Allan Ramsay's masterwork, *The Gentle Shepherd*. Ramsay often visited his friend, John Forbes, at Newhall and this was a source of great pride to Brown. Nevertheless, he considerably altered the building that Ramsay would have known

(colour p.55). Brown, his own architect, added a Gothic porch, drawing room and set a painting of the members of the *Worthies Club* (friends and patrons of Ramsay), by William Aikman, into the library ceiling. In 1852, David Bryce reoriented, extended and baronialised the house to form a T-plan with conically roofed entrance tower and pepperpot turrets. He also refitted the interior. The garden is landscaped to lead into walks along the ravine of the North Esk; on the western walk at Habbie's Howe is the thatched *Rustick Hut*, **Mary's Bower**. Two obelisk **memorials**: one to Allan Ramsay, 1810, the other to Thomas Dunmore (Brown's grandfather), 1794. Other well-preserved landscape features include the walled garden with decorated gateway, U-plan steading and pond with cascade.

NEWBATTLE

Newbotle grew up beside its famous Abbey where, in the mid-16th century, the Earls of Lothian replaced the monks. By the late 18th century *the village of Newbattle which was once very populous has been left to languish*, partly because farmland was being absorbed into the pleasure grounds of Newbattle Abbey. Fortunes changed again the following century with mill development, although most, including Newbattle Paper Mill, have now been demolished, the remainder converted into houses.

Newbattle Parish Church, Abbey Road, 1727-9, Alexander McGill

A harled, T-plan church with its belfry to the street, very similar to Carrington Church. The original paired entrance doors have been filled in and the way in is now through the former vestry. Much altered in the 19th century to accommodate extra congregation. In 1851 two new galleries were added: the north gallery,

Allan Ramsay's most popular poetry was vernacular. The hugely successful *The Gentle Shepherd*, 1725, is his only play and is a pastoral romance concerning the love of shepherds Patie and Roger for Peggy and Jenny. Ultimately Patie is discovered to be of noble birth and restored to his landed position as Sir William Worthy. The play captured the popular imagination:

> *Gae farer up the burn to Habbie's*
> *How*
> *Where a' the sweets of Spring and*
> *Simmer grow*
> *Between twa birks, out o'er a little*
> *lin*
> *The water fa's and makes a sing and*
> *din.*
> *A pool, breast-deep, beneath as clear*
> *as glass,*
> *Kisses wi' easy whirls the bord'ring*
> *grass.*
> Allan Ramsay, *The Gentle Shepherd*

Top left *Newhall in the 18th century*. Above *Newhall*

Newbattle Paper Mill opened in 1820 as Robert Craig & Sons Ltd. It was famous for its coloured papers and lasted until 1890. The hamlet of **Lothianbridge**, which sits at the foot of Glenesk Viaduct, developed around it in the 1850s and 1860s, with larger, detached houses for more highly skilled workers.

Newbattle Paper Mill

Top and above *Newbattle Parish Church*. Right *Newbattle House*

Despite the completion of the church fabric, the internal finishings took some time. In 1750 the Marquess of Lothian wrote in exasperation to the Presbytery of Dalkeith: *The Church of Newbattle having Layn for a great number of years in great disorder without seats And as it is for the interest of all concerned to have it Divided I have given you this trouble begging that the Presbytery would appoint a day for the Division of said Church.* Statistical Account

Newbattle Abbey, c.1810

supported on iron shafts, was extended in 1875 to accommodate miners from the new pit at Newtongrange; the south gallery was removed in 1937. The Lothian loft, though extended in 1859, still has its pilastered wooden frame, *c.*1700. In 1927 the north aisle wall was covered with bright green marble in celebration of the building's bicentenary, the rest in 1938. A remarkable number of the original fittings survive including the upper part of the Corinthian-pilastered, 17th-century pulpit and iron mort-bell, 1616 (both brought from the old parish church), two pewter communion plates with stools, long-handled wooden collection boxes, early communion tokens and so on. The stables have been converted into a hall and the **churchyard** has good 17th-century gravestones including the Welsh family monument: an amazing, ornament-encrusted table.

Newbattle House, Abbey Road, from early 17th century
Originally the manse for the old parish church, it has been extended rather than significantly altered. Rich, orange-harled house with small windows with roll-moulded margins and thick walls. Behind is a five-bay extension with painted margins, 1812-20. When the church was embellished with marble, the manse was not forgotten and was given marble chimney-pieces. Now a private dwelling.

Newbattle Abbey, from 1140
Founded by the Cistercians, the Abbey was at the centre of a thriving business empire which included coal-mining in the Monklands of Lanarkshire, sheep-farming and salt-panning at Prestonpans. The lay brothers' quarters were built first, in the west range; the church in the late 12th century. Evidence of the plan of

RCAHMS

this great monastic powerhouse can be seen around the present buildings where, after the excavation of 1878-95, the outlines of the buildings discovered were laid out in gravel outside and with inlay on the parquet floors inside. After a raid by the English army in 1385, part of the Abbey was rebuilt, including the amazingly preserved quadripartite-vaulted undercroft of the dorter in the east cloisters which has been incorporated into the house. After the Reformation part of the cloister buildings was converted into what must have been a magnificent courtyard mansion, c.1580, by the last commendator, Mark Kerr, who had made a timely conversion to Protestantism.

On the first floor, a 17th-century armorial and architrave with the Lothian sunburst motif, which once decorated the exterior wall of the courtyard, have been absorbed into the interior. In the 18th century, Newbattle became a treasure-house and castellations were added to the entrance front. William Burn added an attic storey, 1836, with dormers and Jacobean gables on the flanking bays of the garden front. In 1858 David Bryce built a family wing at the rear, adding a tower and further extending the block in 18(75). He redesigned the staircase following excavation of the Abbey's crypt (refectory?) below. Yet more additions were made in 18(86) including the addition of the porch.

Thomas Bonnar created one of Scotland's greatest rooms when he redecorated the double-height drawing room, c.1870, which survives as the most splendid example of this style of Scottish decoration. Complementing the dazzling painted coved ceiling above, the walls were given D R Hay's patent imitation damask wall treatment and then hung with the Marquess of Lothian's important picture collection, now elsewhere. The new chapel, 1900, incorporated a 16th-century font found in

After turning out the monks, Mark Kerr and his eldest son *did so metamorphose the building that it cannot be known that ever did it belong to the church, by reason of the fair new fabrick and stately edifices built thereon; except only that the old name and walls of the precinct stand; but instead of the monks, has succeeded the deer* wrote Sir John Scot of Scotstarvet.

Left *Newbattle Abbey in the 1890s.* Below *Drawing-room ceiling.* Bottom *Undercroft*

RCAHMS

RCAHMS

D R Hay patented a paint effect that simulated expensive fabric wall coverings and Bonnar used this at Newbattle. *The ground comprises a thickened paint which, before it is set, was combed with steel graining combs to imitate a woven fabric. This was then painted and the damask pattern was stencilled over this with a paint which dried both to a flat or matt finish and which incorporates sand to provide a texture. The virtuoso effect of this illusionism is completed by the applied gilt fillet masking the non-existent lines of tacks that would secure a real damask.* Ian Gow, *Scottish Society for Art History Yearbook,* 1988

Sundial

Tis an old Building, *but finely situated among the most agreeable Walks and Rows of Trees, all full grown, and is particularly to be mention'd for the nicest, and best chosen Collection of Pictures of any House I have seen in Scotland: The Particulars are too many to enter into a Description of them. The Statues and Busts are also very fine; and there are the most Pictures of particular Families and Persons, as well of the Royal Families of France and England, as of Scotland also, that are, I believe, not only in England, but in any Palace in Europe.*
Daniel Defoe

the grounds of Mavisbank in 1873. The library was created in 1878 by W E Nesfield as two connected, oak-lined rooms with early 17th-century plaster ceilings.

In 1957 the 11th Marquess gifted Newbattle for conversion into a residential adult education centre. The residential wing, 1968, Robert Matthew, Johnson-Marshall & Partners, is on the site of Bryce's kitchen range.

Port Lodges, early 18th century, Alexander McGill
The Abbey's handsome, axial entrance to an avenue that once ran from here to the **King's Gate** (now separated by a housing estate), whose proud date panel of 1822 records its construction for George IV's visit. Square lodges with corner obelisks and balustraded parapets linked by later quadrant colonnades to the original rusticated gatepiers. Their magnificent, sadly crumbling, urns have recently been removed, hopefully only temporarily. For the disused west lodge see Newmills Road, Dalkeith.

A mid-18th-century, classical orangery in the policies was converted in the 19th century into a fernery, now without its glass roof, and a grotto at the entrance to a brick-lined icehouse. Single-span **Maiden Bridge**, 15th century, to the north. Superb twin octagonal **sundials** with obelisk finials, 1635, were moved from the front of the house to the back and given fancy pedestals in the 19th century. In 1873 the **stables** were extended by Bryce with a bargeboard-gabled coachman's house (now converted into houses); beside the **old bridge** (from 16th century?), two ashlar arches with worn armorial panels stand next to its 1956 replacement. Pyramid-capped gates to Newtongrange House (see Newtongrange).

Port Lodges

Left *Newbattle Bridge under construction with the old bridge behind*. Below *Archbishop Leighton's House*

Only a section, to the east side of Newbattle Road, survives of the medieval **Monkland Wall** which once surrounded the Abbey.

Archbishop Leighton's House, 17th century Much-altered house, originally harled, of three storeys which was entered at first-floor level by a forestair. In the 19th century the floor levels were changed to reduce the house to two storeys, the west elevation was rebuilt and the ground level raised. During recent restoration work the upper part of the original door was found, complete with key. After the conversion of the Abbey into a house, the old parish church was built next to Archbishop Leighton's House. This church is now gone but the site was used for some time as the Lothian burial vault. Although the house is within the Abbey policies, the connection with Leighton, who was Bishop of Newbattle from 1641 to 1653, is unproven though the date is feasible.

Archbishop Leighton was also Bishop of Dunblane. When he left Newbattle to become Principal of Edinburgh University, he gave the parish 31 books which, in 1967, were transferred to the Leighton Library, Dunblane. In 1670 he was made Bishop of Glasgow but, wearying of the dispute between the Presbyterians and the established church, he resigned in 1674 and

Below *Glenesk Viaduct*. Bottom *20 Abbey Road*

Glenesk Viaduct, 1847, John Miller Dramatically sited in relation to the road, spanning both it and the North Esk, constructed for the North British Railway to carry the Waverley route from Edinburgh to Hawick. Twenty-three segmental arches on brick voussoirs whose ashlar piers have been braced with old rails. Strengthened with steel to counteract mining subsidence, Thomas Beeching proved a stronger threat and the viaduct was closed in 1969. Repaired in 1993.

20 Abbey Road, 1697, James Chirnsyde The Sun Inn (loyally named after the sunburst of the Lothian family crest) was conveniently sited at the Abbey gates as the first stage out of Edinburgh on the Galashiels road. It has a rear

Main Street

St Anne's

forestair, a large, oval window above the entrance but is no longer an inn. A resited stone (from the Abbey?) on its gable wall forms a drop of fruit and flowers in high relief.

NEWTONGRANGE
Once the Lady Victoria Colliery had been sunk in 1890, Newtongrange grew to be Scotland's largest mining village. The Lady Victoria (named after the Marquess of Lothian's wife) was closed in 1981 but has been preserved as the Scottish Mining Museum. The village remains remarkably intact, every sturdy brick terrace evoking its past; yet it is in danger of being loved too well. Recent *environmental improvements* have fussily landscaped the focal area between the church and swimming pool, all the more unfortunate since Newtongrange already had a communal recreation space in its beautifully maintained public park (part of the northwards expansion of the village in the 1920s). Until very recently, the main post-war addition to the main street has been the **swimming pool**, 1965, W A Bruce Robertson, but infill began on Main Street in 1983 with the **St Anne's** housing scheme, 1982, Rowand Anderson Partnership for the Castle Rock Housing Association, a well-planned grouping of deeply pitched-roofed houses.

Lady Victoria Colliery, 1890-4
Most intact model colliery complex of its date in Europe. Founded by Archibald Hood who, at the age of 67 with a lifetime of entrepreneurial

Newtongrange

mining activity behind him, began the Lothian Coal Company in 1890, in partnership with the Marquess of Lothian. It combined the collieries of Newbattle and Rosewell. **Lingerwood Colliery** (demolished) predated Hood's pit and ran concurrently for a while. Landmark **winding tower**, 1893, William Arrol & Co. The Lady Victoria was one of the earliest pits to make significant use of electricity. Built, as was the rest of the village, with bricks from the Lothian Coal Company's brickworks. The showpiece pit's buildings are red brick skinned with steel frames and roof trusses. The façades are graced with decorative blind-arched windows, rolled margins and, on the winding engine house, yellow brick dressings. The latter happily still contains the 2400hp winding engine, 1894, the largest steam engine surviving in Scotland. The manager's office, 1873, has the Marquess of Lothian's coronet on its datestone and a later porch, possibly contemporary with the wings to the rear, c.1890 (colour p.56). *Open to the public*

The Square, 1914

Parallel rows of single-storey brick houses slope down towards the main street. Halfway up the grid, between **First** and **Fourth Streets**, is this generous grassed lung with beautiful views towards the Pentlands. The larger houses were for the pit managers.

Lingerwood Cottages, c.1870

Two terraces of paired, single-storey, L-plan cottages turn the corner to Lingerwood Road in a smooth curve. Rubble built for the earlier Lingerwood Pit in contrast to the brick rows erected once the Newbattle Brickworks was in production.

Sixth Street, c.1895

One of several built by the Lothian Coal Company, more decorative than the earlier rows. The front gardens were a mixed blessing because in the 1920s, miners' pay was deducted if they did not keep them neat. Baths were installed in the houses in the 1930s, the first in the village. Newtongrange's streets were unnamed until given their functional titles in 1912. **Newtongrange Primary School**, 1925, fits well into the street line, a low block with splayed pilasters punctuating the façade.

Top *Winding Tower.*
Above *Lingerwood Cottages*

Lady Victoria's landmark brick chimney has twice been trimmed down for safety reasons. The overhead gantry that crosses the main road linked the pithead baths, only built in 1954, to the colliery.

Monkswood

Above *Picture House*. Right *Parish Church*

Monkswood, 37-42 Main Street, 1872
Attractive terrace of two-storey red brick
houses, with deep front gardens, these were
managers' houses for the Lingerwood Pit.
Decoratively detailed with contrasting yellow
brick margins and bracketed eaves (colour
p.56).

Newtongrange Parish Church, Main Street,
1942, A Murray Hardie
Sloped shoulders, as at Rosewell Parish Church,
swoop down from the narrow tower to root firmly
in a broad base giving a great sense of solidity.
The fresh, green-tiled roof is a complementing
foil to the surrounding streets of brick. Side
elevations are enlivened by small, stepped flying
buttresses (colour p.56). A contemporary, harled,
church hall to rear. In 1915, Hardie designed the
Picture House, a big harled block (now shops)
at the junction with the A7.

Gorebridge Co-operative Society Buildings,
Station Road, 1908
Substantial terrace with shops below, some
with original fronts, accommodation above.
Carved panel of hands proudly clasped in
united endeavour. Gables decorated with
stylised gunloops.

Dean Tavern, Main Street, 1910,
A Murray Hardie
Subdued Arts & Crafts, half-timbered with a
single-storey extension, 1962, to the front and a
spacious interior refitted at this time too. Set
up by the colliery, its profits were used towards
supplying electricity and a park for the village.
It is still a *Gothenburg* (see Black Bull,
Dalkeith). Also for miners' diversion, the harled
brick **Newtongrange Institute**, 1911, had a

Dean Tavern

John 'Cocky' Romans, the self-styled *Laird of Newtongrange*, built Romans' Buildings on the Loan in defiance of the Marquess of Lothian who owned the land around his smallholding. In the late 19th century, he built himself a huge, modern mansion, **Newtongrange House** (demolished *c*.1930): *a somewhat pretentious and eccentric mansion.*
Third Statistical Account

Abbey Inn

Abbey Inn, Main Street, 1874
Diminutive, Gothic corner block with carved date panel inscribed *JR* for John Romans, builder of what was once a three-storey block of shops; the gable end of the upper storey of *Romans' Buildings* bore a large statue of a monk on a pedestal. Subsequently lowered and licensed in 1897.

At **Easthouses**, the Bogwood housing scheme, 1925, accommodated miners from West Lothian and Lanarkshire who had found work in the Easthouses and Newtongrange pits. In Bogwood Road, **Easthouses Parish Church**, 1954, Alan Reiach. Clean lines in traditional materials, white harl and pantiles with a rubble bell tower (colour p.56).

Easthouses Parish Church

37 **Cockpen Old Parish Church**,
from 12th century?
Ruins of the earliest church in Midlothian whose building periods are visible but difficult to date. It seems as if a wall was added at the east end in the 13th century re-using fragments of a 12th-century, chevron-patterned doorway. The belfry was added in the 17th century, as was the **Dalhousie vault** in which 19th-century lead coffins covered with decorative studded leather were recently discovered. When John Knox's brother William was minister here, he helped the Presbytery of Dalkeith to remove altars and some sculpture from Rosslyn Chapel. An 18th-century tablestone to an unknown minister portrays the man himself, though not on the slab but tucked between its legs, whiling away eternity with a book.

Cockpen Old Parish Church,
Alexander Archer, 1834

Cockpen New Parish Church, 1818-20,
Archibald Elliot
Cruciform, restrained Gothic revival built by
R & R Dickson to replace the Old Parish Church
whose bell, 1680, was moved here. A landmark on
its sloping site, the tall, half-engaged west tower
forms a porch and is crowned with octagonal
corner pinnacles. The Dicksons economically
repeated the design at Kilconquhar (see *The
Kingdom of Fife* in this series). Refitted internally,
1886, by Peddie & Kinnear, who left the Gothic
fronts on the galleries but replaced the pews.
Above is a delicate plaster vault (colour p.90).

38 **Kirkhill House**, 1828, Thomas Hamilton
Hamilton extended a plain, 18th-century house
with a tower and a single-storey bay to create
an Italianate villa whose strong, boxy geometry
has been impaired by the extension upwards of
the southern block. The square tower, the most
sophisticated element of the design, has
become less prominent for the same reason.
Hamilton characteristically grouped the
chimney-stacks on the tower, using them as
part of the parapet and carrying their line up
from the row of blind windows through the
eaves cornice. A cast-iron balcony runs along
the south elevation. Now a hotel.

Top *Cockpen New Parish Church.*
Above *Kirkhill House*

Right *Dalhousie Courte.* Below
Octagonal tower, Dalhousie Courte

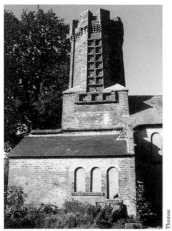

Above and left *Arniston House*

Top *Newbyres Row, Gorebridge.*
Middle *Main Street, Gorebridge.*
Above *Cockpen New Parish Church.*
Top right *Dalhousie Castle.*
Right *Dalhousie Courte*

James Gardiner

James Gardiner

Above *View towards the Pentlands from Gorebridge.* Left *James Gardiner Associates, formerly Carrington Parish Church*

Above *Old Parish Church, Temple.*
Right *Bonnyrigg Primary School*

Dalhousie Courte, late 18th century
Boldly extended with showy detail, *c*.1880, by
John Dennis (a Newcastle builder) for himself.
His Italianate tower and corner turret loom
large over the earlier house and have been
cement rendered. Inside, the window margins
have inset mirrored panels which throw light
into the principal rooms (colour p.90). Behind,
is a brick stable block with a castellated,
octagonal (doocot?) tower. Internally altered for
use as a hotel, a glass function room replacing
the original conservatory in the 1970s. Also
known as **Brixwold** (see p.88). Nearby is
Cockpen Nursery School, mid-19th
century?, lozenge glazed with a trio of Tudor-
gabled dormers and schoolhouse adjacent.

Dalhousie Castle

39 **Dalhousie Castle**, from 15th century
The L-shaped tower that lies within the heart
of the present building was transformed into a
Scottish Renaissance mansion, probably when
Lord Ramsay was created Earl of Dalhousie in
1633; his initials and those of his wife are on
resited pediments on the south-west curtain
wall. He hedged his bets by retaining the
curtain wall (now much restored). Other
reminders of its defensive past are the tall slits
above the west entrance which took the gaffs of
the drawbridge when it was raised from the
moat (now filled in) and the drum tower which
contains the well. The vaulted chambers of the
tower's basement are intact, but the floors
above have been rebuilt. Gradually, the tower
was swallowed up by additions which

Dalhousie Castle

James Ramsay, later Governor-General of India, related to his mother, Countess of Dalhousie, the progress of William Burn's work at the castle: *It now looks like a doocote owing to the holes cut to ventilate the roofs* but that later on *the drawing room ceiling is old fashioned and accords very well with the character of the house*, 1830.
Dalhousie Muniments, Scottish Record Office

eventually covered the courtyard inside the curtain wall. John Douglas *mangled the castle* in the 18th century, according to Sir Walter Scott. Perhaps George Paterson, architect, who is recorded as *repairing and extending* in the 1780s, was carrying out Douglas' earlier scheme. He certainly fitted out the circular rooms in the drum tower.

William Burn suited Sir Walter better, *restoring and repairing in the old taste* in 1825 with mullion and transomed windows, Gothic interiors and the building up and castellating of the curtain wall. His spectacular entrance hall has an elaborate traceried ceiling with circular inset lanterns above a mezzanine landing reached by a brass balustered double stair. He fitted a cast-iron Gothic main stair and created a suite of south-facing, grand reception rooms; the dining room with a dark, flat timber ceiling, the drawing room with a Jacobean plaster ceiling and twin marble chimney-pieces and the library with heavy rococo ceiling which collides with Gothic bookcases, perhaps fitted later. The top storey burnt out in 1867. The vaulted armoury, with iron-doored chamber adjacent, was converted into a billiard room with a staircase down into it, possibly by David Bryce, and is now a chapel. The house was also completely redecorated by Morison & Co, 1875. The wooded policies were landscaped in picturesque manner as extensive and romantic pleasure grounds, *c.*1750, by James Robertson. Replanting has smothered the scheme including the avenue which once led to the circular, decorative laundry. An arched bridge forms a scenic approach to the castle. The walled gardens, *c.*1807, by Walter Nicol, are derelict. After being run as a school it has, from 1985, been a hotel (colour p.90).

Entrance Hall

GOREBRIDGE

Commanding some of the loveliest views in Midlothian with an uninterrupted vista of the Pentlands, housing schemes surround a wonderfully intact 19th-century core. Gorebridge is distinct from the village of Arniston to the north, though their boundaries have merged somewhere along Hunterfield Road (colour p.91).

Founded by the Dewars of Vogrie in the early 1800s, Gorebridge became a busy shopping centre later in the century. Its thriving gunpowder manufactory, **Stobs Mills**, 1794-1875 (mostly demolished), was eventually superseded by coal-mining. The village grew dramatically following the opening of the railway station, 1847, and the sinking of the Emily Pit, 1854, and the Gore Pit, 1878. For his miners, Robert Dundas of Arniston provided various local amenities, most of them marked with initial panels. Extensive housing on the periphery began at the west end of **Hunterfield Road** with semi-detached, flatted houses, 1927, James Cairns. A major council house building programme started to the east of Gorebridge in the 1950s for incoming miners working at Bilston and Monktonhall pits. Private development has taken over from the 1980s.

With a lucrative Government contract to supply gunpowder for the Napoleonic Wars, Stobs Mills expanded to an area of over three-quarters of a mile and became a major employer in the area. Accidents were inevitable. The works were surrounded by artificial mounds so that *when an explosion does occur, it seldom destroys any other building than that in which it originated (New Statistical Account, 1845).* What happened to the workers is not recorded.

With the attraction of Arniston Glen and improved railway links, Gorebridge became a holiday resort: *this year (1897) a large number of visitors have taken furnished apartments for the season and the village presents an unwonted bustling appearance.*

I remember when there was nothing but a bare hillside with a double row of houses which looked like a couple of barracks. That was in 1830 but there has been a large extension since then which was consequent upon the extension of the railway and we now have a village of 1300 odd inhabitants.
Robert Dundas, *Dalkeith Advertiser*, 1894

RCAHMS/Gorebridge Local History Society

Left *Main Street in 1895.*
Below *32-34 Main Street*

The curved slope of **Main Street** is an unspoilt monument to late 19th-century commercialism evoking the time when business was so good that, from 1901, many shopkeepers refronted their premises, and moved from living over the shop to new houses on **Private Road** (colour p.90). **Nos 38-40** have broad, arched windows at ground floor and have been subdivided from a single shop. Many of the well-detailed fronts have date panels, such as the substantial **post office**, 1879,

Thomas

In Gorebridge, many houses have not a whole pane left and the roofs present a most picturesque appearance; some entirely unroofed on one side, and from most of the others the tiles are removed so as somewhat to resemble a sieve.
Report of an explosion at Stobs Mills, *Edinburgh Advertiser*, 1825

Below *Newbyres Castle*. Middle *Former Gorebridge Free Church*. Bottom *Dundas plaque, 13 Hunterfield Road*. Right *13 Hunterfield Road*

or initial panels such as **Nos 32-34**, 1889, which is inscribed J P (James Pendreich, grocer). At the bottom of the hill, a solid little fortress **Bank of Scotland**, 1980, Bamber Gray. **Stobs Mills House**, *c*.1795, belonged to William Hitchener, part owner of Stobs Mills.

Newbyres Cottage, early 19th century
Sturdy remnant of the original village, with pantiles, an etched glass inner door and a large stable onto the street. It is one of several buildings named after the 16th-century **Newbyres Castle** which stood to the west of Main Street (demolished 1963).

Newbyres Hall, Hunterfield Road, 1858
Originally the Free Church, Robert Dundas bought it when the new church opened opposite, rendering it redundant, and had it extended to the back in 1882 as a public hall. A disfiguring 20th-century extension to the road now masks the entrance. The new **Gorebridge Free Church**, now **Gorebridge Christian Fellowship**, 1882, MacGibbon & Ross, used to have a spire, now only the bellcote remains.

No 13 Hunterfield Road, 1886
Robert Dundas built this gabled cottage as a public library (for books originally donated by Dr Milne of the gunpowder mill) and village club; one quatrefoil panel reads *RD*, another bears a lion rampant. Now a private house.
No 34, 1889, built in a cottage style for the district nurse, has turned wooden finials and a panel with an illustration of *Time Flies*.

The plain, little **Hunterfield Tavern**, 1911, built by the Arniston Coal Company, is still a *Gothenburg* (see also Black Bull, Dalkeith & Dean Tavern, Newtongrange). Its hefty profits paid for a cinema in the 1920s and the **Arniston Welfare Park**, 1930. At the brow of Hunterfield Road is **Gorebridge Parish**

Church, 1884-5, Hardy & Wight, and nearby a trio of gable-porched cottages, **Newbyres Row**, 1886, the centre one with a thistle finial (colour p.90).

ARNISTON

The 1845 Emily and Gore Pits at Arniston Engine have been demolished but in **Engine Road**, **Emily Bank**, a pair of overseers' houses in red and yellow brick is a vestige of the group. The red brick **public laundry**, 1895, was built for the miners by Robert Dundas: *I hope it may prove to be a source of comfort for the workmen's families*, and is now converted into three houses. On the outskirts is the Queen Anne style **Newtonloan Lodge**, 1890, James Jerdan once a fever hospital, converted to a senior citizens' home in 1953. Designed with two isolation ward wings, only one was built leaving six beds to cope with anticipated epidemics.

40 **Arniston House**, from 1726, William Adam Defiantly grand home built on the site of Old Arniston House by Robert Dundas who, in 1725, was forced to resign from the post of Lord Advocate having disagreed with Walpole. He may have chosen Adam having admired his work at Mavisbank, which was being built at the time. Unfinished when Dundas died in 1753, work started again under the supervision of William Adam's son, John. Originally, the ashlar centrepiece of the otherwise harled grand show front had a rusticated, three-bay basement with round-arched openings but this is now obscured by the north porch added in 1877 by Wardrop & Reid who also heightened the colonnaded links by a storey. The magnificent, galleried entrance hall has a joyous baroque plasterwork ceiling, completed in the 1730s, by Joseph Enzer; its integral clock, 1592, was removed from the courtyard of Old Arniston House and reinstated here in a new case custom-made in 1738 by Francis Brodie, Edinburgh's premier 18th-century cabinet-maker (colour p.89).

RCAHMS/Gorebridge Local History Society

Top *Emily Bank, Emily Pit opposite.*
Above *Newtonloan Lodge, c.1920*

The old Manor-house of Arnistoun *was situated exactly where the present house stands; the Oak-room and vaults beneath, being part of the old building. The vault beneath the east end of the Oak-room was the parlour or eating room of my great-grandfather, Lord Arniston. The Oak-room was then divided into two appartments, one a dining-room used only on great days, and the other the principal bedroom for strangers of distinction visiting the family.*
Arniston Memoirs

Despite his political conflicts, Robert Dundas was far from isolated in his new home: *At Arniston for a number of years he kept what would now be called open house, where friends and neighbours came uninvited and met with cordial welcome and for many years he had entire command of the shire of Midlothian, living with the freeholders like brothers and doing them every service in his power.*
Alexander Allardyce, Scotland and Scotsmen in the Eighteenth Century, 1888

Arniston House

RCAHMS

Arniston House

RCAHMS

Francis Brodie was *employed by some of the best families in this part of the kingdom*. William Adam recommended him to the Duke of Hamilton as *the best man in town, I doubt if anyone else will do*. He also fathered the infamous Deacon Brodie who was hanged for theft in 1788.

Also at a very great expense he *formed the cascade in the Gardener's Park, which was let off when he and his guests sat down to dinner and continued to run for about an hour. The aqueduct which filled the reservoir pond at the top of the bank, was brought off by a dam immediately beneath the junction of the Deanhead and Castleton burns. I just recollect the taking down of this cascade sometime about 1764 when the present garden was made by my father. The steps and stages of the cascade, resembling that at Chatsworth, were of stone, and the appearance of the white water, tumbling down from one to the other, is still fresh in my recollection. The water fell into the pond which is now in the middle of the garden, and thence by a sluice into its natural channel near the Grotto.*
Arniston Memoirs

Walled garden loggia

Thomas

The west range became the dining room and drawing room instead of the double-height apartments William Adam had intended. Gutted following attack by dry-rot in the 1950s, the rooms are currently being restored by Nicholas Groves-Raines. During 1754-8 additions included a stable, roofed with slates from Shank House, in the court behind the east pavilion and an orangery behind the west pavilion. The oak parlour was extended with the addition of the glazed, south entrance, c.1800, and a new library was created on the principal floor in the 19th century superseding the splendid original library which was, as was usual at that time, at the top of the house. The latter has remained essentially intact having found a new use; the bookcases now house porcelain.

Parts of the formal **landscape** designed by William Adam in 1726 are still visible today, and while the cascade to the south has gone, the wilderness area and remnants of the avenues, whose vistas were designed to close on elements in the landscape beyond, such as Arthur's Seat, survive.

The informal parkland of the early 19th-century layout is largely what exists today. The grotto to the north of the 18th-century **walled garden** may incorporate stones from Old Arniston House; one is dated 1644. The walled garden loggia and ornamental doorways and bridges were added to the pleasure grounds in 1808 and incorporate pieces saved from the destruction of Edinburgh's Parliament House including the Royal Arms which were mischievously set into the south pediment on the garden front of the house. The gable of the **gardener's house**, c.1764, which faces the walled garden, has a tall, blind Gothic window and signatures of its successive occupants carved in the reveal of an upstairs window. In 1753, the Shank estate was incorporated into the pleasure grounds.

The ruins of **Shank House**, 17th century?, survive as well as the walls of its extensive garden which has a place in Scottish garden history as it was while he was a gardener here that John Reid wrote *The Scots Gard'ner*, 1683. The family tradition of rescuing architectural sculpture continued with the salvage of what are now the South or **Cougar gates**, *c.*1766, erected here 1824, whose wide rusticated banded piers are topped with recumbent beasts. The **north lodges** and gates, from 1790, bear a lion, the Dundas family crest, and an elephant, the Oliphant crest. **Braidwood Bridge** is inscribed *Robert Dundas of Arniston, Chief Baron of the Exchequer 1811* and was rebuilt in the 1930s. The original Braidwood Bridge, 1754, is at Carrington Mill.

Top *Shank House.* Above *North lodge.* Left *Carrington*

Dundas explained his rescue of the Cougar gates thus: *The pillars of that gate with the two lions on the top of them, stood in front of Mr Mitchelson's, afterwards Dr Bennet's house, in Nicolson Street, and were purchased by me for twenty guineas. They were erected when I was a boy at the High School about 1766 or 1767, and it was one of the first houses in that street.*
Arniston Memoirs

CARRINGTON

Charming, sleepy hamlet of single-storey, pantiled, rubble cottages. Built to serve **Carrington Mains**, a model farm with classical detailing and intact range of outbuildings added in 1813 as a result of a local programme of agricultural improvements initiated by the Earl of Rosebery, principal landowner in the area. A branch of the family lived at Rosebery House nearby.

One side of the street is essentially unchanged, though many of the cottages have been paired. On the other, the church is flanked by local authority housing, 1938-50, cottages to one side, more modern development to the other. **Primrose Gardens** has ideal-home fashion-plate dwellings, with swept gables and immaculate front gardens. For a short while after 1703, the parish was renamed Primrose after the newly created Viscount Primrose, Earl of Rosebery.

Below *Carrington Mains.* Bottom *Primrose Gardens*

Carrington Parish Church

Rosebery improvements to their
Midlothian farms (including
**Aikendean, Cauldhall, Capielaw,
Edgelaw** as well as **Carrington
Mains**) consisted of commissioning
Richard Crichton to design ranges of
new estate buildings and
encouraging better land
management. The farmer at
Carrington Barns was a shining
example: *On the farm of Carrington
Barns, the present tenant has given
much encouragement towards
emulation in ploughing, building of
stacks &c. The whole farm is
drained the good effects of which are
manifest from the very heavy crops
of oats, barley &c. on the ground.
Many other farms on the Earl of
Rosebery's estate are also partially
and as may be expected will ere long
be thoroughly drained where
required. Of late years, the whole
surface has undergone a great
change towards improvement.*
New Statistical Account, 1845
Right *Temple.* Below *Headstone at
Whitehill Aisle*

Carrington Parish Church, 1710
T-plan church with sundials at its southern
corners and a doocot in the tower which is in
the centre of the streetward elevation. In 1838
Thomas Brown removed the harling and
replaced the high, loft-illuminating windows
with larger, pointed lights with Y-branched
tracery. Contemporary session house at the
gate. The church was converted, successfully
retaining its external integrity, into an office in
the 1980s by Crichton Lang, Willis & Galloway
for James Gardiner Associates who designed
their airy, mezzanined interior (colour p.91).
The former manse, **Carrington Hill**, 1756, is a
smart, two-storey house which has grown
wings, two in the mid-19th century, a third in
the 1970s.

41 **Whitehill Aisle**, 18th century
In an idyllic setting at the end of a hedged,
grass path through nearby fields is the burial
place of the Ramsays of Whitehill, on the site
of Carrington's old parish church, **St
Kentigern**, founded in 1243. The plain box
aisle has fallen into disrepair but some
wonderfully decorated 18th-century
headstones have survived intact.

TEMPLE
A quiet, sequestered, little place which, from the
early 12th century, was the Scottish
headquarters of the Knights Templar,
Balantradoch, around which they held a great
deal of land. The village consists of one street,
Main Street, with primarily 18th-century
cottages. **No 21** is probably the earliest, dated
1760, and has TB and a compass and set-square
carved on its lintel. **Nos 25-27** were built the
following year. **No 35** is dated 1785 and has
been extended to two storeys, while at **No 14**, a
plaque records *Sir William G Gillies, Painter,
1898-1973, lived and worked in this house.* At

the far end is a resolutely suburban housing scheme of four blocks completed in 1961 and the **United Free Church**, 1844, with its gable end to the street, open belfry and little carved trefoil with a tree of life. Converted, 1964, as the **Tradoch Hall** and restored, 1994, retaining its coloured glass windows.

The Order of the Temple was founded to protect pilgrims in the Holy Land against attack by the Saracens for which they were rewarded with gifts of land back in England and Scotland. The Order was suppressed in 1312 and the lands given to the Order of St John of Jerusalem, which cared for the sick (see *West Lothian* in this series). Residents of Temple funded them with a tenth of their income.

Above *Tradoch Hall*. Left *Old Parish Church*

Old Parish Church, early 14th century
At the heart of an exquisitely picturesque grouping in a riverside glade below Temple village this small roofless church is the only surviving Templar building in Scotland. After 1312, when the Order was suppressed, the church passed to the Knights of St John. The walls and parts of the late Gothic tracery are intact with animal-stopped hood moulds. The east end with sedilia is mostly original but its gable belfry was added during the rebuilding of the west end in the 17th century, the bell's ropemarks are visible in the stone. Below is a carved inscription, emphasised with lead: VAESAC MIHM, which has eluded antiquarians but may stand for *Vienne Sacrum Militibus Johannis Hierosolymitani Melitensibus* (The Sacred Council of Vienne, to the Knights of St John of Jerusalem and Malta). On the east wall is a **monument**, 1831, to Charles Hitchener of Stobs Mills gunpowder works (see Gorebridge). Conserved by Simpson & Brown, 1980-2. The graveyard has interesting early stones including a touching memorial to farmer John Craig who died 1742 and is shown in his Sunday best with his children. The Revd Goldie's stone records his charitable donations since *the last of his race, he survived all his relations* (colour p.92).

Midlothian's industrial boom affected one of Temple's idyllic aspects: *Formerly salmon and sea trout came up* (the South Esk) *for spawning; since the erection, however, of dam-heads, &c. for carrying on various manufactories, farther down the rivers, their ascent in this direction has been entirely prevented.*
New Statistical Account, 1845

John Craig's headstone

Shillinghill, 1832, Thomas Brown
Built as Temple Parish Church, Gothic revival replaced the real thing, overlooking it from the

Above *Temple House gateway.* Right *Shillinghill, before conversion, and the Old Manse*

In 1700, **George Home of Kimmerghame** found Rosebery *very large being a body double and two long jambs or wings single. It fronts north west the second story is very noble the drawing room taking up the 2d and 3d story up to the roof and finely painted above he has a French man painting other Roomes the great fault of the house is that it has not a fine staircase. I find Dalmeny has throun doun one that was in the midle of the House and designes to built it up again but it will be ane eyesore breaking the view betwixt the 2 wings after all it is a cold place of the Country and a cold house.*

Below *Rosebery House.* Bottom *Rosebery steading*

slope opposite. Sensitively converted to domestic use in 1977 though a prominent conservatory has since been added. The session house, contemporary with the church, was originally an offering house so that money did not sully the church itself.

Old Manse, from 17th century
Seems to have grown from part of the (north cloister?) buildings of the Templars' establishment, possibly from 12th century. Repaired c.1802, extended and jollied up with bargeboards in 1890, it is being restored. Nearby **mill house** dates from 1710.

Temple House gateway, 17th century
Isolated, at the east of the village, its context demolished, it comprises an arch with alternating courses of projecting rusticated blocks and chevron ornament. Temple House was purchased, in a derelict condition, by the Dundas family in 1761. (Were some of the 18th-century cottages built from its rubble?)

42 **Rosebery House**, from late 17th century?
It may be that there is an early core in this much-altered house. Certainly, the simple box **lodge**, late 17th century, is related to Clerkington House, the earlier seat here. The house is plain, largely 19th century?; Sydney Mitchell & Wilson designed various stupendous replacements in 1913 to no avail. The Gothic episcopal **chapel**, 1913, was intended for use by visiting clergy, a purpose disapproved of by the Bishop who refused to allow its consecration. The extraordinary **Rosebery steading**, c.1805, is in late 17th-century style, as are the pyramid-capped gatepiers to the main house which were probably added at this time. The steading has capped screen walls with castellated pavilion fronts and a clock tower which is also a doocot. A further court was added by 1855.

[43] **Fountainside** farm has a good sheephouse. These little temples with their sturdy columns and roofed courts, though not unique to Midlothian, were once particularly common here. This is one of the survivors. Why they should have such grand supports is not clear (colour p.109).

Above *Rosebery House lodge*. Left *The opening of Gladhouse Reservoir*

Archibald Primrose, 5th Earl of Rosebery, succeeded Gladstone as Prime Minister in 1894. At Rosebery, he created a lending library for the local area, shelving out the lodge and installing books which are now at Dalmeny House (see *West Lothian* in this series).

Gladhouse

Service buildings for Gladhouse Reservoir, an artificial loch engineered by Messrs Leslie by damming the South Esk. Opened in 1879 it was intended to increase the water supply available for the Edinburgh area to 39 gallons per person. A weir, pumping house and metal bridge survive.

Gladhouse is wholly an artificial loch, an immense embankment being thrown across the South Esk, and a reservoir thus formed in the glen with an area of 400 acres, and a storage capacity of 1700 million gallons. The embankment is a truly great work, and constructed on the large scale necessary when such an immense body of water is to be controlled . . . (When the Lord Provost performed the opening ceremony) *about a hundred and eighty gentlemen were assembled and the company afterwards partook of dinner in a large shed which had been decorated for the occasion at Gladhouses.*
Illustrated London News, 1879
Below *Toxside Schoolhouse*.
Bottom *Toxside Farm*

Gladhouse Villa, *c*.1879

Baronial home of the reservoir caretaker, which has a board room for the Reservoir Committee with bulrush and waterlily cornice on the first floor. Municipal pride required ornate finishing with square crowstepped tower and decorative relief panel above the entrance.

Toxside Schoolhouse, 1847,
Thomas Turnbull

Austerely functional, built to serve the local farming community by the heritors of the parish and in operation until 1956. Children of all ages were taught in a single room on the ground floor, the teacher lived above. The Revd James Goldie *who for the long period of 58 years was Minister of the Parish* is commemorated on a large inscribed plaque.

[44] **Toxside Farm**, *c*.1870

Surprisingly decorative, in pattern-book villa style with bargeboards and pretty, columned porch. The steading behind is advanced at the corners so that, on approaching, they read as pavilions for the house.

Hirendean Castle

Bonnar, George Meikle Kemp's biographer, wrote of Moorfoot Farm: *Nothing now remains of the village of Moorfoot but a picturesque farmhouse, with its quaint gables, and here and there, exposed above the turf, clusters of low ruined walls, the rugged surfaces of which are clothed with moss and ferns . . . It is a solitary place, with a grave, solemn beauty, and a fit birthplace for such a genius as Kemp.* Although Kemp was not born here, his family moved to Moorfoot after he had left home.

45 **Hirendean Castle**, 16th century?
At the wild, southern tip of Midlothian with its sheep-grazed plains ringed by the Moorfoot Hills, a rubble ruin (once an outpost for the monks of Newbattle Abbey) clings to the slope of Hirendean Hill (colour p.112). At the
46 entrance to **Moorfoot Farm** is a sturdy little building (17th century?), thick walled, deep roofed and variously extended, which was once thought to have been the birthplace of George Meikle Kemp, architect of the Scott Monument (see *Edinburgh* in this series).

COUSLAND
The village was for centuries a lime-producing centre. In 1557, Edinburgh contracted the *lyme men of Cousland for furnessing lyme to the wallis of the toun*. It thrived in the 19th century with the proximity of the Portland Cement works. The ruins of the late 16th-century **Cousland Castle** stand within an enclosure (once a garden or orchard), now the centrepiece of a housing estate. The village has a well-maintained, corrugated-iron **village hall**, *c.*1950, a fast-disappearing breed.

Top *Moorfoot Farm*. Above *Cousland Castle*. Right *Cousland Smiddy*

Cousland Smiddy, 31 Hadfast Road, from late 18th century
Miraculously preserved, pantiled smiddy complete with anvils, late 19th-century bellows and full range of tools, which has been saved from becoming a fossilised time-capsule through its continued use as a wrought-iron workshop. Originally associated with local farms such as **Northfield** (which has intact, pantiled ranges). Repaired during the 19th century but essentially unchanged other than by a small 1940s extension housing an engineering workshop. The Cousland Smiddy Preservation Trust hopes to repair and develop it further (colour p.110). *Open to the public by appointment*

Cranston Parish Church, 1824
Gothic revival parish church in the Oxenfoord
policies near the stables. Rebuilt after a fire,
1861, by Wardrop. A sundial, 1797, on a south
buttress records the restoration of the earliest
church on the site. Galleried interior with
lovely, Gothic-script bordered, patterned
stained glass. Dalrymple aisle to the north,
extended late 19th century. In a co-operative
division of resources for the spiritual well-being
of the parish, Sir John Dalrymple paid for the
building of the church and William Callander
for the resiting of the former manse, **Cranston
House**, from beside the gates of his home to a
more convenient site near the church. It is not
clear whether the result is a conversion of
Alexander Stevens' planned building, 1793-5,
or dates from c.1824. Double L-plan Jacobean
with barn, stable and walled garden. Now a
private house.

Cranston Parish Church

If Boswell is to be believed, Old
Oxenfoord Castle was certainly in
need of modernisation. *We supped
and went to bed in ancient rooms,
which would have better suited the
climate of Italy in summer than that
of Scotland in the month of November.*
James Boswell, 1786

Above *Old Oxenfoord Castle.*
Left *Oxenfoord Castle*

47 **Oxenfoord Castle**, 1782, Robert Adam
An early example of Adam's innovative castle-
style in which the 16th-century L-shaped tower
of Old Oxenfoord Castle was encased in a
sophisticated interpretation of Scotland's
fortified past. The extent of the original tower
is marked out with high corner turrets,
extended from the original bartizans, which
break through the crenellated parapet, while
the corners of the new castle are finished with
small, once pepperpotted, bartizans. A
stringcourse loops over round-headed windows
at ground-floor level contrasting with the
primarily square-headed fenestration of the
upper levels and echoing the curves of the
recessed arches. Over the entrance are
reclining beasts, an ox and a horse.

Adam's dining room was formed from the
existing principal room of the old castle but with
the west wall extended into a bow. He fitted 10
bedrooms into a compact area using the corner
turrets as dressing rooms. The bedrooms in the
middle of the west side were equipped with

Adam's contemporaries viewed
his transformation of Oxenfoord as
restoration rather than rebuild: *Sir
John gave the improvement of the
castle to Mr Adam who with his
usual wonderful degree of invention
preserved all the old rooms and by
some additions but with hardly any
alterations, turned all former
awkwardness into sources of
convenience and picturesque beauty.*
An Account of Oxenfoord Castle

Garden front, Oxenfoord Castle

Sir John Dalrymple wrote an influential treatise, *An Essay on Landscape Gardening,* 1774, exploring his preference for the *Romantic* rather than the *Beautiful.* His landscaping at Oxenfoord was remodelled in the 1840s.

Oxenfoord Home Farm

Midlothian District Council

Perhaps it would be a difficult matter to find another residence for a man of fortune in the whole country . . . in all respects so truly pleasant and agreeable. Taste has ornamented and industry cultivated the country for several miles round, and in all directions, to such a degree, as to render it a residence extremely delightful.
Preston Hall described in *Picture of Edinburgh,* 1806

Preston Hall, c.1800

adjoining powdering rooms in the bow. His plans show that at first he intended to continue using the turnpike stair but eventually opted for a cantilevered staircase. At some point before 1840, a bay window was added to the garden front thereby spoiling its symmetry and reducing the prominence of the towers. William Burn swamped Adam's work with his additions of 1840-2 which provided more scope for formal entertaining by the new Earl of Stair. He provided the large porch and double suite of grand reception rooms on the south side comprising a library and drawing room, the decorative schemes of which have survived largely intact. Burn ran a new front along the east entrance façade and in doing so lessened the grandeur of its trio of recessed arches and the dramatic tension between bold horizontal and vertical elements. From 1931 to 1994 the castle was home to Oxenfoord Castle School.

Oxenfoord Bridge, *c.*1783

Carries the drive to the castle across a deep gulley on three symmetrical arches with a castellated parapet. Probably by Alexander Stevens though his proposed plan shows a plain parapet and higher central span. It seems likely that Burn added the castellated **north lodge** and crowstepped **stables**, *c.*1840-2, while he was working on the castle.
Oxenfoord Home Farm at Chesterhill relates to the 18th-century building phase and has a perfect Georgian farmhouse.

48 **Preston Hall**, 1791-1800, Robert Mitchell Refined, classical house with an imposingly long elevation consisting of a main block connected to balustraded pavilions by three-bay links on the (present) garden front and by quadrant links on the entrance front. After making his fortune with the East India

RCAHMS

Left *Stair hall*. Below *Lion gates*

Company, Alexander Callander decided to retire in 1789 and instructed his agent to buy **Old Preston Hall**. Despite having been altered by William Adam, *c.*1740, it was largely demolished and work began on his perfect retirement home but he died in 1795, leaving his brother to finish this apogee of Georgian aspiration. Economically, Adam's wings were retained (though recast) complete with bold, marble chimney-pieces. The perron (external stair) may be Adam's too (colour pp.109,111).

In 1832 the house was reoriented, the entrance moved to the north front and a porch added. The cool, north façade of the main block contrasts with the decorative south façade which has Coade Stone ornament, figures of ancient and classical warriors reclining atop the linking bays and pretty tempietto crowns on the flanking pavilions. Inside, the principal rooms are grouped around an imposing top-lit, double-height hall with first-floor gallery. The hall's neoclassical decoration was diluted with Watteauesque painted ornament by David Roberts in the 1830s. The drawing room was also decorated with painted ornament, in this case by Wallace & McFarlane, 1860.

Much survives in the grounds, probably all designed by Robert Mitchell, *c.*1795. The bell-roofed tempietto was moved by Sir John Callander from the south garden to top the unfinished octagonal **mausoleum** intended for his brother (colour p.109). The imposing **lion gates** have paired, cubed lodges flanked by balustraded screen walls and symmetrical wrought-iron gates between columns supporting recumbent lions. The **stables**, *c.*1795, are quadrangular; the west front has pedimented pavilions with windows in recessed arches and a pedimented central entrance to courtyard. Twin octagonal brick **gazebos**, *c.*1795, rise up from the west wall of the walled garden.

Preston Dene, 1891, John Kinross
Built for the factor of the Preston Hall estate in a happy conflation of Arts & Crafts and Queen Anne with a sprinkling of 17th-century Scottish detailing. Smartly finished inside with decorative plasterwork and with the generous fenestration typical of Kinross (colour p.110).

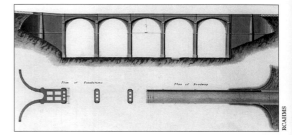

Lothian Bridge

Lothian Bridge, 1827-31, Thomas Telford
Commissioned by Sir John Dalrymple, when he was the spirited convener of roads for this district, to cross the Tyne at Pathhead because increasing traffic on this major route south rendered the small crossing at Ford impractical. Engineering elegance in five, 80-ft-high arches of 50-ft span. As with the Dean Bridge (see *Edinburgh* in this series), footpaths are carried on segmented arches.

Below The Hald. Bottom 71-77 Main Street

PATHHEAD
Long ribbon of houses which was, in the 18th century, a succession of almost identical, single-storey thatched cottages. Individualism ran riot a century later in an engaging display of ingenious adaptation. Recent pavement widening has improved life beside the busy A68, though the choice of herringbone bricks is not ideal.

The Hald, *c.*1935?
The village was expanded in the 1930s, to the south with bungalows, to the north with a council development, but The Hald is the most innovative addition. Asymmetric, white-harled with swooping gables, etiolated windows and pantiled roof (colour p.112).

Main Street
While many of the late 18th-century houses have been altered, some good examples remain,

James Gardiner

James Gardiner

Thomas

Thomas

Top *Sheephouse, Fountainside.*
Middle *Mausoleum at Preston Hall.*
Above *Preston Hall.* Top left
Crichton Castle. Left *Ford*

Top *Cousland Smiddy.* Above
Crichton Limekilns. Right *Crichton
Mains.* Bottom *Preston Dene*

RCAHMS

Thomas

Above *Borthwick Parish Church*.
Left *Borthwick Castle*. Below
Preston Hall

Thomas

James Gardiner

Thomas

Thomas

Top *Hirendean Castle.* Above *The Hald, Pathhead.* Right *Sheriffhall Farm*

particularly **No 47** and the two-storey run from **Nos 71-77**. **No 7** has been given a gabled doorpiece with star finial and gablet skewputts. **Nos 40-46** are recent, competent infill with contrasting harling and grey, painted margins. **No 57**, Grays House, was built up to two storeys in 1876 and the new level given raised window margins; the same builder was at work on **No 107** in 1877. In the same year, **No 81** was extended to the dizzy height of three storeys and the triple dormers given fancy iron finials for good measure. **No 87** kept its feet on the ground, its lintel is inscribed 1760. The Royal Bank of Scotland at **No 91** has a little neoclassical façade while **Nos 113-115** were rebuilt in the 1920s with big box dormers and canted bay windows hiding under the eaves.

91 Main Street

149 & 151 Main Street

Agnesville, No 149, late 19th century
Set back from the road and, though single storey, given every elaboration namely gablet skewputts, canted central dormer with iron finial, large doorpiece, tiny iron gates to the front and side and decorated hoppers; replacement windows are a jarring note.

The 19th-century modernisation of **No 151** is skin-deep because above its new parapeted front, its chimney-stack has a prominent thackstane, a reminder that it, like the rest of the village, would originally have been thatched. The local builder excelled himself at **No 169** which has an extraordinary carved doorpiece. **Craigerne**, No 187, is the best of the 1930s bungalows beyond. The little, 19th-century Tudor **primary school** has a later bellcote, 1903. The 1876 **Gospel Hall** began life as a masonic lodge and had a range built adjacent, 1897, with masonic symbols on its lintels. The hall has thin obelisks at its corners and a plaque proclaiming its former use.

169 Main Street

At the village of Ford lives James Small, the best plough-maker in Scotland. In this particular department, indeed, he is perhaps second to none in the land. He makes 300, 400, sometimes 500 ploughs in a year.
Statistical Account, 1793

FORD

Bypassed by the main road following the construction of Lothian Bridge, the village fell *much into decay* but now it nestles in tidy repose within its little hollow in the Tyne valley. It has lost its church but retains its perfect laird's house and 18th-century, three-storey, three-bay **Mill House** (colour p.109).

Ford House, 1680

A remarkably untouched house built by a cadet branch of the Frasers of Lovat; L-plan within a walled garden. Octagonal turnpike stair in the re-entrant angle, lovely ogee slated roof and rich ochre harling. Restored with verve by Mary Tindall, 1956, while retaining the original panelling and doors.

Dowery House, from 17th century

Roughly Z-shaped expansion from the original tower, a three-bay, L-shaped block with crenellated, bowed end added in early 19th century. Crenellated screen wall attempts to regularise the entrance front by masking the tower. Rebuilt internally in 1901 when it became the dower house for Vogrie House. Now has sombre, dark drydash.

Edgehead Windmill, late 18th century

The solid, round tower retains its character though the conical roof has long since lost its sails and windows have been inserted for its conversion to domestic use. Platform-roofed extension to the side with delicate lead cresting, *c.*1955. **Edgehead** village has a breezy, open aspect. It steps down the north-western slope of the Tyne valley into **Chesterhill** in a succession of three-bay cottages, some with their harling, some without. There is a colourful array of roofing materials from orange pantiles to purple-grey slates.

Top *Ford House*. Middle *The Dowery House*. Above *Edgehead Windmill in 1924*. Right *Edgehead*

Opposite:
Anti-clockwise from top left *Vogrie House; Stables; Entrance hall; Dewartown; No 54*

DEWARTOWN

Vogrie estate village which was, in 1839, *the neatest looking village in the Parish*. Until recently, it comprised a row of rubble cottages running down just one side of the street. Now houses are being put up all along the opposite side. **No 20** is inscribed *Time Cottage 1783*; **No 8**, 1884, is of two storeys; **Nos 50** and **54** have ashlar fronts, rusticated corner stones and Gothic windows, 1823; **No 18** has charming, naïve 18th-century neoclassical panels flanking the door and other embellishments.

The houses are ranged in one line along the road – *the opposite side being occupied by a small plantation, along which a copious stream of pure water flows at all times, supplying the inhabitants with the means of cleanliness and comfort, and adding much to the pleasant and healthful appearance of the place. There is now no part of the parish where a greater number of children may be observed enjoying the sports of the evening, and giving an animated air to the village.*
New Statistical Account, 1845

49 **Vogrie House**, 1875, Andrew Heiton II
A dazzlingly original structure in a municipal setting. Dewar, the Perth whisky magnate, chose a Perth architect for his big new home. Baronial meets Arts & Crafts outside; largely Gothic inside. Heavy massing is counterpointed by a wonderfully detailed roofscape with delicate iron finials, conical slated roofs, sturdy chimneys and deeply overhanging, fretted bargeboards. Innovative fenestration of the windows of the upper storeys where fixed, unglazed, astragalled upper sashes have plate-glass behind which creates effects of light and shadow, particularly when seen from below, and provides a transition from the sparely detailed, plate-glass-windowed ground floor to the excitement of the roofline. A glazed porch attached to the west front replaces a later veranda. Used as the Royal Edinburgh Hospital for Mental & Nervous Disorders from 1924 to 1963 when it was taken over by Midlothian District Council. The Gothic **stables**, *c.*1825, repay negotiation of the large shed which unfortunately obscures

The New Statistical Account says that they [the stables] *are 'Built in a style of taste and splendour indicating what the proprietor would have done to the house had his scheme been completed'. Whatever the house was like, it is indeed a relief that Heiton's tough masterpiece did not replace anything so irresponsibly happy as the stables.*
Colin McWilliam

North lodge

Southside Castle

Alderdean

them from the house. A canted screen-wall joins the U-plan in front of the pretty, crocketed octagonal tower. Conversion to a guide hostel has necessitated iron fire-escapes on the entrance façade. *Gardens open to the public*

Some distance from the house is the brick **walled garden** complete with mid-19th-century glasshouses. The **lodges**, west and north, 1896, are bargeboarded to echo the house, the west entrance has good wrought-iron railings.

50 **Southside Castle**, *c.*1640

Tall, L-plan laird's house which underwent major alterations in the mid-19th century. This included reducing the structure from four to three storeys by changing the floor levels. A new staircase and entrance were constructed in the re-entrant angle and mullioned, crowstepped dormers added. A scale-and-platt stair led to the first-floor principal rooms while a turnpike stair continued to the private chambers. The vaulted lower storey survives as do the multiple corner turrets, though they have been extended to hold their own against the dormers. Lintel inscribed *1640-4*.

Alderdean, 1995, Hope & Co

Large new addition to the edge of the old village of **Newlandrig** has an Arts & Crafts air. Deeply pitched red roof, tiled dormers and prominently splayed, buttressed chimney. The landing window to the rear has a projecting canopy recalling a Dutch barn. At the other end of the village is **Newlandburn**, a three-bay Georgian villa with asymmetrical wings, which sits in a Gertrude Jekyll garden.

Crichton Castle, from late 14th century

Remains of rude magnificence, redolent of their colourful medieval occupants; cultured, powerful and constantly falling in and out of royal favour. On an isolated plateau overlooking the Tyne valley, on what was the principal route south, Crichton was soon joined by Borthwick Castle on the opposite side but, unlike its neighbour, the massive original tower was greatly extended and became one of Scotland's finest Renaissance houses (colour p.109).

The tower became the centre of the east range of a spacious courtyard house when ranges to the south and west were added, to join with the original north ancillary block, by

RCAHMS

Crichton Castle

The estates of Crichton were built up by William Crichton, Chancellor of James I and Master of the Royal Household but the castle stayed in the family for only three generations. The 3rd Lord Crichton plotted against the king and his estates were confiscated in 1484. The most infamous resident was the 4th Earl of Bothwell, husband of Mary Queen of Scots, who, after the murder of Lord Darnley, fled with her not to his own home but to the greater stronghold of Borthwick Castle in 1567. Crichton's most remarkable occupant, Francis Stewart, inherited the title in 1581, newly returned from Europe and steeped in culture though with a zest for living that finally went too far. He forfeited the estate after a mercurial change in fortunes. Accused of plotting with witches to destroy the King he subsequently proceeded to attack him at Holyroodhouse in 1590, then tried to kidnap him at Falkland and finally fled to Naples, dying in poverty. His son was reinstated but had inherited a taste for luxury and fell so far into debt that, in 1649, the estate was bought by Hepburn of Humbie and Crichton became ruinous soon after.

Chancellor Crichton, probably in the 1440s at the height of his power. The south range, with its deep machicolated parapet, was his principal *lodging* and contained the main entrance, now blocked in, to the castle courtyard. The Chancellor's apartment began on the first floor and was reached by a forestair inside the courtyard. The great hall was built in conjunction with the west range which housed the kitchen and accommodation for retinue and visitors on four floors above, each with a connecting door to the *lodging* adjacent. The real splendour of Crichton lies in the exuberant Renaissance additions carried out during its modernisation, 1581-91, by Francis Stewart, newly created Earl of Bothwell. The courtyard elevation of the north range is unique in Scotland, a seven-bay arcade carrying dazzlingly crisp diamonds of nailhead-faceted masonry, something Stewart would have seen on his travels to Italy but which he translated into a Scottish idiom. The ashlar palace front contrasts with the freestone of the old tower, emphasising the Earl's elevated status as Lord High Admiral of Scotland, and includes ropework decoration and rosettes. Inside, he installed Scotland's first scale-and-platt staircase, a revolutionary introduction in a country of spiral stairs. The exterior has been designed for effect with a series of large windows marching along the entire front below a decoratively treated corbelled cornice at wallhead level. The Admiral also built ancillary buildings to the south of the castle. The sole remnant, with its arched entrance, may have been a stable. Its buttresses are a later reinforcement. *Open to the public; guidebook available*

RCAHMS

North range

Sir Walter Scott described Crichton in *Marmion*, 1822:
*Nor wholly yet has time defaced
Thy lordly gallery fair;
Nor yet the stony cord unbraced,
Whose twisted knots, with roses laced,
Adorn thy ruin'd stair.
Still rises unimpair'd below
The courtyard's graceful portico
Above its cornice, row and row
Of fair hewn facets richly show
Their pointed diamond form.*

Collegiate churches were founded by wealthy patrons so that clergy could pray exclusively and constantly for their salvation, usually within sight of the object of their devotions. Approximately 38 were built in Scotland before the Reformation, many on the sites of earlier churches, seemingly unfinished; it appears that often only the choirs were completed since they were all that were required.

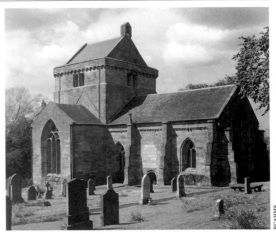

Right *Crichton Parish Church.*
Below *Crichton Parish Church, c.1852*

Crichton House

Crichton Parish Church, from 1449

Stocky, cruciform church with square tower at the crossing and dramatic interior. Sir William Crichton adapted the earlier parish church on the approach to his home as the Collegiate Church of St Mary and St Kentigern in order that his soul could be prayed for on a regular basis. The choir was rebuilt for the purpose and the nave allowed to decay. The transepts are later; the line of their predecessors can be seen on the tower. The choir's cornice is decorated with naïvely carved faces, more potato-heads than grotesques. Inside, the carving is more sophisticated with ogival heads to the sedilia, piscina and sacrament house. The muscular interior has pointed, barrel vaults over the choir and transepts and steep, pointed crossing arches which thrust upwards from low-springing points. Rebuilt, *c.*1825-45, to seat 600, perhaps over-optimistically since *its distant situation excludes the hope of any such number attending regularly*. Renovated internally, 1898, by Hardy & Wight, who removed the box pews. No longer in use, it is administered by the Crichton Collegiate Church Trust. *Open by appointment*

51 **Crichton House**, *c.*1650

A more domestic-scaled seat than its predecessor, for the Laird of Crichton. Three-storey, harled L-plan with an octagonal turret with turnpike stair in the re-entrant angle and an 18th-century wing to the south. The garden was the first in Scotland to be laid out in a *French* manner by James Justice (author of the

Scots Gardiners Directory, 1754), who also installed a *pineapple stove*, designed by Richard Cooper. Restored by John Gibbons.

CRICHTON

Primarily a farming settlement near the castle. **Crichton Mains**, 1885-7, Sir Robert Rowand Anderson, is an accomplished foray into Arts & Crafts by an architect better known for his public commissions such as the Scottish National Portrait Gallery (see *Edinburgh* in this series). Beautifully constructed, it relies on massing rather than detailing for effect (colour p.110). **Crichton Cottages**, 1885, probably also by Anderson, once housed farm workers for Crichton Mains. Random rubble cottages with Tudor elements, gabled end bays and pointed pend arch with drying green hidden decorously behind. **Crichton Limekilns** nearby are fairly intact and one of Midlothian's best surviving examples (colour p.110).

Borthwick Castle, *c*.1430

A stately and most magnificent castle, this is a splendid medieval survivor. Built by Sir William Borthwick, with dispensation from James I, it is a big bruiser of a building; its massive U-plan main block rising a breathtaking six storeys to 110ft. Nonetheless, it displays an impressive

Crichton Cottages

Above *Borthwick Castle, Alexander Archer, 1834*. Left *Borthwick Castle*

Cromwell addressed the 8th Lord Borthwick: *Sir, I thought fit to send this trumpet to you to let you know, that if you please to walk away with your company, and deliver the house to such as I shall send to receive it, you shall have liberty to carry off your arms and goods, and such other necessaries as you have. You harboured such parties in your house as have basely and inhumanely murdered our men; if you necessitate me to bend my cannon against you, you must expect what I doubt you will not be pleased with. I expect your present answer and rest your servant.*
O Cromwell, 18 Nov. 1650

Great hall

Mary Queen of Scots and the hated Lord Bothwell (see Crichton Castle), who had just murdered her husband, Lord Darnley, fled from Holyroodhouse to Borthwick in 1567 where they narrowly avoided capture by the rebel barons. The castle's hospitable hall thus became a focus of romantic speculation: *In pacing through the solitude of this august room, the image of Queen Mary, feasting with her unworthy and guilty Bothwell, startled from revelry by the voice of insurrection, and finally obliged to escape in the guise of a page, comes before us.*
John Dickson, 1894

A recent study of the 60 masons' marks on the walls at Borthwick suggests *that the tower house is a homogenous building throughout, excepting only minor alterations, everything is original . . . twenty masons at least were engaged with the carving of the (hall) vault's ashlar.*
J Zeune, 1992

Borthwick aisle in 1980

finesse of design. The principal rooms occupied the main block while the wings accommodated retainers and service quarters with vaulted ceilings at every level and a complex arrangement of interconnecting stairs. The high construction quality of its fine ashlar walls and stone-slabbed roofs has ensured its longevity though partly damaged by Cromwell under siege; the east elevation is still scarred from this spat – the most attractive theory for the breach in its shell.

The entrance was originally at first-floor level on the north side and was reached by a bridge from the curtain wall, now gone except for a small section which is of rubble with wide gunloops. The basement is entered separately at ground level and is connected by a turnpike stair to the guardroom above. The magnificent great hall has a pointed tunnel vault, once covered with painted decoration, huge hooded fireplace and is largely as it was left by the Borthwicks when they abandoned it in the 17th century. By the next century it was *the seat of a colony of jackdaws* but was saved from further dereliction when it was sympathetically restored in the 1890s by John Watherston & Sons. The machicolated wallhead parapet was repaired, the gateway replaced, though on its original site, the guard tower adjacent rebuilt, a new external stair added and the timber hall screen with minstrel gallery above reinstated. The castle's strength continued to be of value because during the Second World War various national treasures were moved here for safety. Converted to hotel in 1973 (colour p.111).

Borthwick Parish Church, 1862-4, Brown & Wardrop
Old Borthwick Church, 12th century, was burnt out in 1775. Plans to restore it were shelved though Thomas Brown incorporated its apse and south chancel wall into a Gothic-revival church, as well as the south transept and barrel-vaulted **Dundas of Arniston burial aisle**, the latter having been converted from the medieval sacristy in the early 17th century. The tall, broach spire of his church contrasts strikingly with the blocked mass of the castle behind. The **Borthwick aisle**, 15th century, once housed the tomb, *c.*1470, of the 1st Lord Borthwick who is in full armour and lies beside his wife. Traces of the original paint survive on the figures whose garments are

sculpted in fascinating detail down to the armour rivets. The canopy of the monument was largely recarved in the 19th century when the effigies were moved from the apse; they are on the move again, temporarily resited in the nave (colour p.111).

In a particularly pretty part of the Tyne valley, Borthwick is within sight of Crichton Castle to the east. Adjacent to the charming, former **schoolhouse** is the plain Tudor **manse**, 1850, with walled garden incorporating stones from Old Borthwick Church.

Currie House, from late 17th century
Organically extended from an original L-plan, built from the stones of a former Currie House, and said to have been an inn for sightseers at Borthwick Castle. The principal extensions are a Georgian wing, 1815, and a two-storey block, 1870s. Harled with an open timber porch and 19th-century dormers it is *embosomed amidst its sheltering woods* still with a *pleasing aspect of rural retreat and comfort* (*New Statistical Account*, 1845). The walled garden may be 18th-century.

Borthwick Parish Church

The 1861 rebuild of Borthwick Church was paid for by David Kidd, owner of Inveresk paper mills and inventor of the gummed envelope. He wanted to provide a *nice church for Borthwick* as a memorial to his parents. His father was overseer at Arniston House for 16 years.

TYNEHEAD
On the longest summit in Britain, the tiny village once served the mainline Tynehead Station, now closed, though at its heart **Tynehead Farm**, *c.*1850, is still worked. A lovely grouping with original brick stack it was altered by the Prestonhall Estate Office in 1907.

Above *Currie House*. Left *Tynehead Farm*

Garden front, Middleton Hall, in the 18th century

52 **Middleton Hall**, from 1710
Originally a neat, six-bay, harled house of the highest quality in *quiet and genteel seclusion.* Though gradually extended outwards, it is still a fine building in a delightful, wooded setting. Entrance and garden fronts have segmental pediments with puny urns. The pavilions were added in the late 18th century and attached to the main block with single-storey, straight

RCAHMS

RCAHMS

Top *Middleton Hall.* Above *Hall*

Landscaping work at Middleton Hall was not without its problems: *The proprietors have repeatedly attempted to enhance the beauty of this locality by forming a pond in the centre of the ornamented grounds – but the site being in the course of the stream which passes behind the mansion house, has been found insufficient to resist the mass of water which occasionally pours from the streamlets of the moorland – and which has repeatedly borne all before it – and descended through the neighbouring valley, not without risk of considerable damage and danger to the inhabitants. It is not likely that the attempt to construct a pond will be repeated, nor is it desirable, though a great additional beauty to the grounds has thus been rendered impossible to be realised. New Statistical Account, 1845*

Right *Cakemuir Castle.* Below *Esperston Limekilns and cottages*

RCAHMS

links which were raised by a storey in 1898 by J MacIntyre Henry for the head of Moss Empires. He also balustraded the wall in front of the house, added a ballroom, refitted the interior with extensive panelling and early 18th-century-style chimney-pieces and provided a stable court. Converted into a conference centre and extended to the west, in 1962, by Stanley Ross-Smith. Both the house and pattern-book lodge, late 19th century, are currently empty.

53 Esperston Limekilns

These most dramatic of Midlothian's many limekilns, which supplied the building trade as well as farmers, were demolished in 1992. The massive range of four kilns was brick-lined and connected by a tunnel at the rear. A pretty row of associated cottages seems lost without its context.

Midlothian District Council

54 Cakemuir Castle, c.1560

At the top of the four-storey tower is a prominent parapet on which two covered recesses for guards on watch survive, one with its stone seat intact. The stair tower is finished with a caphouse and, unusually, none of the floors is vaulted. Some 17th-century pine panelling survives. The large wing to the south-west was added in the 18th century by Henry Wauchope, Secretary to Lord Bute, and the windows were enlarged during this time of less pressing defensive constraints. It was restored as a summer retreat from Edinburgh in the late 19th century and during its light baronialisation the Georgian wing grew curvy dormer gables. Modernised by Rowand Anderson Paul & Partners, 1926, and again by Neil & Hurd in the 1950s.

Cakemuir Castle, Alexander Archer, 1839

FALA

Fala rests comfortably on the northern foothills of the Lammermuirs. Though it was just *a few miserable cottages* in 1792 it developed rapidly in the next century when its famous blacksmith and popular coaching inn at neighbouring **Blackshiels** ensured a constant trade for the local population. The A68 runs close by, the route designed by Thomas Telford in 1834 to speed the mail coaches between Edinburgh and Lauder, but at a sufficient distance to leave the village still in the state of *seasoned age and respectability* described by its contented minister a century ago.

The churchyard was not always so peaceful: *In 1820 when the grave-robbing business was booming there were two bodies taken from Fala and so a Committee of Watchers was set up to patrol the graveyard at night with a blunderbuss and on one occasion 'the Watchers thought they had done a great deed; in the darkness they had fired on and scared off what they conceived to be graveyard thieves, but next morning it was found that the minister's goat had been badly wounded'.*
Fala and Soutra Past and Present, 1987

Blackshiels Inn, from 17th century
On the main road at the turning to Fala. With its adjacent steading it operated as an inn until 1880 after which Blackshiels hamlet was absorbed into Fala. On their way south in 1773, after a cold night at Oxenford (see p.105), Johnson and Boswell stayed here, *My friend and I thought we should be more comfortable at the inn at Blackfields.* Crowstepped additions, 19th century, were constructed from the remains of William Adam's **Hamilton Hall**.

Left *Blackshiels Inn*. Below *William Adam's Fala House, also known as Hamilton Hall, was struck by lightning, c.1830, and subsequently demolished*. Bottom *Fala Parish Church*

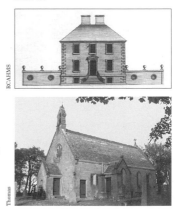

Fala Parish Church, 1865
Possibly a reworking of the former church on the site by David Bryce who was working locally at the time, redesigning Woodcote Park. Small Gothic box with trefoil skewputts and gable belfry. Spectacular views from its hilltop

churchyard down towards the Firth of Forth. Fine farmer's **tablestone**, 1707, with carved harrow and plough and pedestal supports.

Fala Manse, 1792
Commodious, five-bay manse. The first incumbent complained that *the Manse, though new, draws water through every part of the walls and roof exposed to the blast.* Matters improved and single-storey offices were added in 1831, while in 1889 the minister was provided with bathroom facilities in the shape of the Precentor's Tower, a bowed bay at the back. Recently restored, though without its harling, and converted to a private dwelling.

Right Fala Manse. Below Design for Fala UP Manse. Bottom Fala & Soutra Primary School

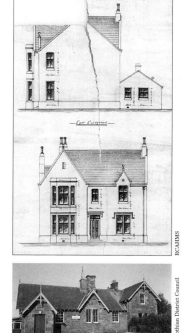

Fala's 18th- and 19th-century cottages ramble up the slope to the church; 1930s suburbia intervening briefly at **No 25** with its high chimneys, bay window and smart stained glass. Of the few larger houses, **No 31**, late 18th century, is still harled with gabled dormers and was probably once Fala's inn, later occupied by its baker. The **village hall** is an ex-army hut moved here in 1919.

Fala House, 1875, Robert Baldie
Economically Tudor, this was the **United Presbyterian Manse** until 1936 when the congregations of the two churches united. It stood near the late 18th-century Secession Church, later the UP Church, which was demolished in 1972.

Fala & Soutra Primary School, 1875
Probably also by Robert Baldie. Deep timber gables with spindly finials relieve the plain exterior. The schoolmaster's house was originally built as part of the school and was enlarged in 1886.

Soutra Aisle, *c*.1164
Stone-roofed, rubble chamber with a barrel
vault commanding a panoramic view over
Midlothian and beyond. A fragment of the
Hospital of the Holy Trinity which was founded
by King Malcolm IV for travellers and the poor,
and richly endowed until funds were transferred
to Trinity College and Hospital (see *Edinburgh*
in this series) after which it was used as the
parish church until 1618. The rest of the
Hospital was demolished in 1850 except for this
part which had been used as the burial place of
the Pringles of Soutra since 1686. Current
research into the DNA of medieval bones from
the site hopes to inform our understanding of
patterns of illness. (Now Borders Region.)

The rugged moorland beyond has been rendered
a less exciting contrast with creeping
afforestation but the change in landscape is still
abrupt enough for the deeply suburban, 1930s
butterfly-plan house on the hill beside **Nether
Brotherton** to surprise. (Now Borders Region.)

Woodcote Park, completed 1977,
James Morris, Morris & Steedman, and
Eleanor Morris
Sleek, glazed house which has adopted the
established wooded setting of David Bryce's 1854
baronial remodelling of its predecessor
(demolished, rot-riddled in 1971). A slender
turret remains, offsetting its replacement,
housing the water tank and ultimately intended
to be for extra accommodation. Designed in 40-ft
units, the house is impeccably finished with
laminated timber beams, bright white marble
and bronze-tinted glass which subtly controls the
light-suffused spaces. A double-height
conservatory with swimming pool leads off the
end and opens into the landscape. The principal
rooms are on the first floor, a conscious reference

Soutra Aisle

***To a traveller coming from the
south**, the view from Soutra is most
enchanting. Passing for a
considerable way through a dreary
moor, where nothing meets the eye
but barren heath; – here all at once
the fine cultivated counties of Mid
and East Lothian, with the Firth of
Forth, and coast of Fife, burst upon
his view. The suddenness of the
change and the mingled group of
hills and dale, and wood and water,
which now stretch extensive to the
eye, give such a throb of pleasure to
the heart as is not to be described.
Statistical Account, 1792*

Nether Brotherton

Below and left *Woodcote Park*

Thomas Somerville's gravestone shows him in the act of teaching his pupils, above them is the sun and an inscription which is said once to have read: *As the sun communicates light to the world so the teacher gives light to his pupil.*

to Scottish tradition. This superb house continues to develop with the recent reshaping of its approach whereby a sense of occasion is created by arriving at an angle via a series of curves.

NEWTON

Farming and industry have co-existed in Newton parish since early times. At **Millerhill** rows of mid-19th-century? miners' cottages (banded with iron, c.1936, to defy subsidence damage) face the c.1840 crowstepped improvement farm steadings of **Newton** and **Longthorn**. Egon Reiss'
56 monolith pithead towers for **Monktonhall Colliery**, 1953, witnessed the departure of the coal industry until successfully restarted in 1993.

57 **Newton Parish Church**, 1742
Built to replace the old parish church whose 17th-century tower, an eye-catcher for Dalkeith House (see p.12), is the only survivor. Deeply droved masonry distracts from the smooth ashlar of the later porches. An exterior stair leads to the miners' gallery, 1742. Gothic-windowed session house, 1742, with sundial and dated gable is attached to the south wall. Internal alterations of 1890 included the incorporation of a little of the earlier inscribed panelling, dated 1732 and 1747. In the

Thomas

RCAHMS

RCAHMS

RCAHMS

In 1725, it was agreed that the miners could build a loft in Newton Old Parish Church though they were required to pay for the gallery and external stair that this necessitated. They had to petition again when the second parish church was erected, although this time, the gallery was erected for them. Resited below it are two carved wooden **panels** painted with inscriptions and trade symbols which were put up by the miners to commemorate both lofts.

churchyard are several early gravestones including a 1775 **tablestone**: a father's touching tribute to a teacher son.

Chalfont, 1803
Georgian manse for Newton Parish Church. Symmetrical, with one-bay, arched-windowed wings, set back from the three-bay front. Front door has a moulded architrave.

Newton House, late 17th century
Seven-bay house acquired in the early 1700s by Lord Edmonston who was developing the local coalfields. Modernised in the early 1800s. In 1855 the house was turned around with a new first-floor entrance with external stair, extended to the back and remodelled internally. An early gas producer, c.1913, was located in a brick outhouse and gas lamps survive in the vaulted basement. Adjacent is a 16th-century circular tower; doocot above, defensible tower with gunloops in its 3½-ft-thick walls below.

58 **Woolmet House**, 1686; demolished
All that remains of this magnificent building is its grand Renaissance **gateway**, with classically detailed piers through which the judiciously sited Danderhall Miners Club is entered. The interior of the house had remained largely untouched, if decayed, until its destruction in 1950. Some of the chimney-pieces are said to have found their way to the Castle of Mey, Caithness.

59 **Sheriffhall Farm doocot**, late 17th century
Pigeons entered by the lantern at the top of the square tower with pyramidal roof and gunloops, originally the stair tower of **Sheriffhall House** (demolished), a Buccleuch property undermined by one of their coalpits (colour page 112).

Top left *Newton Parish Church*. Top *Miners' loft panels*. Middle *Chalfont*. Above *Newton House*

Opposite:
Anti-clockwise from top left *Stair, Woodcote Park; Farm at Millerhill; Cottages at Millerhill; Thomas Somerville's headstone; No 1 Shaft Winding Tower*

Above *Woolmet House.*
Right *Sheriffhall Farm doocot before repair*

I would like to thank Alasdair Anderson, Jimmy Baird, Jean Blades, Alistair Buchanan, Tony Cairns, George Campbell, Mungo Campbell, Sir John and Lady Clerk of Penicuik, Keith Dyble, Major Callandar, Charles Callander, Scott Cooper, Phil Crow, Kitty Cruft, John Dunbar, Richard and Anne Emerson, Anja and James Gardiner, John Gifford, Mr Hall, Mr Kelly, Deborah Mays, Colin McLean, Cameron Manson, Simon Montgomery, Mary Noble, Una Richards, John Sanders, the Sisters of Charity of St Vincent de Paul, Neville Petts, Jacqueline McDonnell, David McKerrachar, Charles McKean, Sam McKinstry, Stuart Maxwell, Alison Shepherd, Mrs Buchanan-Smith, Alison Spence, Deborah Spencer, Neil Stewart, Ben Tindall, David Walker, Liz Whitfeld, Frank Young, Quintin Young and to the countless people I met while travelling around Midlothian who were, without exception, kindly and open spirited.

Thanks also to my colleagues at the RCAHMS, particularly to Ruth Wimberley, Veronica Steele, Victoria Collison Owen, Simon Green, Ian Gow, Lesley Ferguson, Geoffrey Stell and Graham Ritchie for their support, both practical and moral, to Tahra Duncan and Stephen Thomson for their impeccable photographic processing, to all at the RIAS and Rutland Press, especially Helen Leng, and to everyone at Almond Design – Linda Hardwicke, Kirsty Wichary, Dorothy Steedman and John Franchetti.

I am indebted to James Gardiner for his generosity in making so many of his beautiful photographs of Midlothian available through the Open Space Photolibrary, High Street, Edinburgh. Thank you to those who kindly allowed me to reproduce illustrative material: Alasdair Anderson, His Grace the Duke of Buccleuch and Queensberry, Rebecca Bailey, Sir John Clerk of Penicuik, Midlothian District Council, James Darwin, Gorebridge Local History Society, John Hume, Deborah Mays, Philip Mercer, Simon Montgomery, Morris & Steedman, Forgan & Stewart, The Earl of Rosebery, The Hon Francis Hepburne-Scott and John Trotter.

Without Midlothian District Council this would not have been possible. David Smith, Ian J Young, Alan Reid, Scott Ballantyne and Kirsty Towler have been very helpful and I have spent many happy hours in the Local Studies resource at Loanhead benefiting from Marion Richardson's expertise.

And to Sebastian for his encouragement, judgement and ability to keep his sense of humour.

References

Lothian, Colin McWilliam, 1978, is invaluable. Also helpful are the publications of the Gorebridge Local History Society, Dalkeith Local History Society and Midlothian District Library Services, *Country Life* and the various Statistical Accounts. *Inventory of Monuments and Constructions in the Counties of Midlothian and West Lothian*, Royal Commission on the Ancient and Historical Monuments of Scotland, 1929; *Exploring Scotland's Heritage: Lothian and the Borders*, John R Baldwin, 1985; *The Baronial and Ecclesiastical Antiquities of Scotland*, R W Billings, 1852; *Groome's Gazetteer*, 1882; *Gazetteer of Scotland*, 1843; *The Antiquities of Scotland*, Francis Grose, 1797; *From Rosewell to Rhondda*, Archie Blyth, 1994; *The Clerks of Penicuik*, Iain Gordon Brown, 1987; *Midlothian Gravestones*, Islay Donaldson, 1994; *William Adam*, John Gifford, 1989; *The Castellated and Domestic Architecture of Scotland*, David MacGibbon & Thomas Ross, 1887; *The Ruined Castles of Midlothian*, John Dickson, 1894; *The Last Mill on the Esk*, Nigel Watson, 1987; *The Prisoners at Penicuik*, Ian MacDougall, 1989; *Castles and Mansions of the Lothians*, William Paterson, 1883; *The Arniston Memoirs*, George Omond, 1887; *The Annals of Penicuik*, John J Wilson, 1891; *The Lime Industry in the Lothians*, Basil Skinner, 1965; *Rosslyn: its Castle, Chapel and Scenic Lore*, Will Grant; *Loanhead: the Development of a Scottish Burgh*, Robertson Sutherland, 1974; *Cranston: a Parish History*, Revd Dickson, 1907; *The Midlothian Esks and their Associations from Source to Sea*, Thomas Chapman, 1895; *Memoirs of the Life of Sir John Clerk*, ed John M Gray, 1892; *General View of the Agriculture of Midlothian*, G Robertson, 1795; *Tour of the Northern Counties of England*, Thomas Dibdin, 1838; *Scottish Country Houses*, ed Ian Gow and Alistair Rowan, 1995; *A Scottish Man of Feeling*, H W Thomson, 1931; *Handy Guide to Penicuik*, John Thomson, 1911; *Picture of Edinburgh*, 1806; *Fala and Soutra Past and Present*, Daniel and Jean Blades, 1987; *A Tour through the whole Island of Great Britain*, Daniel Defoe, 1724; *An Account of Oxenfoord Castle*, Hew Dalrymple, 1901; *The Country Seat*, Scottish Record Office, GD18/4404/1; *Internationale Archaeologie*, J Zeune, 1992; *The Journal of a Tour to the Hebrides with Samuel Johnson*, James Boswell, 1786. The Alexander Archer collection of topographical views is held in the National Monuments Record of Scotland.

INDEX

GLOSSARY

PICTORIAL GLOSSARY

1. Ashlar (dressed stonework in smooth blocks).
2. Balustrade (line of small columns usually along a balcony or parapet— in this case in ironwork).
3. Bow (projecting semi-circular bay).
4. Buttress (Stone column supporting the walls, usually of a church).
5. Cherry-cocking (small stones set between larger blocks of stone).
6. Corbel (stone supporting a projection above, one end embedded into a wall).
7. Cornice (projecting top of a wall).
8. Crowstepped gable (a gable in the form of a series of steps).
9. Curvilinear gable (wavy-shaped gable).
10. Cupola (roof light).
11. Dormer window (window projecting through the roof plane).
12. Drum tower (circular one-bay tower, usually for staircase).
13. Eaves (overhanging edge of roof).
14. Fanlight (patterned glazed window above a door).
15. Finial (crowning feature e.g. of tower).
16. Keystone (centre stone of an arch).
17. Palazzo (a building in imitation of an Italian Renaissance palace).
18. Pavilion roof (piended, or hipped—sloping on all four sides).
19. Pediment (triangular feature).
20. Pilaster (flattened column attached to a wall).
21. Quoin (long and short protuberant stones emphasising the corner).
22. Stringcourse (stone course or moulding projecting from the surface of the wall).
23. Tracery (window pattern, usually in churches).
24. Venetian window (three-part window, the centrepiece raised and curved).
25. Wallhead or nepus gable (gable rising through the roof in the front of a building).

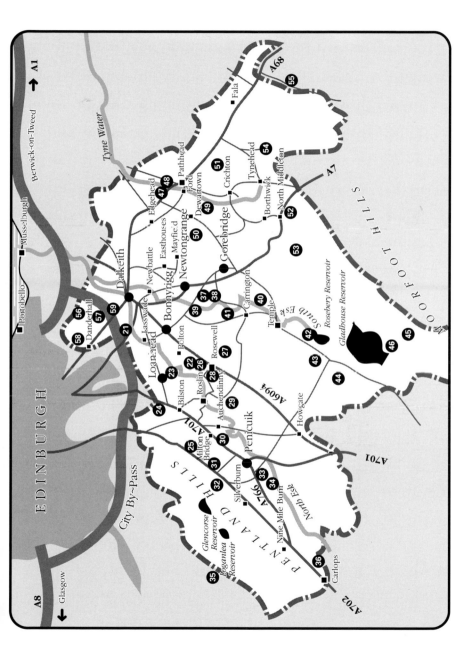

ARCHITECTURAL
— GUIDES —
TO SCOTLAND

A MAD IDEA: the belief that by the millennium the whole of Scotland can be compressed within 31 vivid, pocket-sized volumes, painting the history and character of each place through the medium of its surviving or demolished architecture.

"Good armchair reading with their exotic mixture of fact, anecdote and personal comment"
– Colin McWilliam, *The Scotsman*

SERIES EDITOR: Charles McKean

— *Currently available* —

EDINBURGH by Charles McKean new edition 1992
DUNDEE by Charles McKean and David Walker new edition 1993
STIRLING AND THE TROSSACHS by Charles McKean reprint 1994
ABERDEEN by W A Brogden second edition 1988
THE SOUTH CLYDE ESTUARY by Frank Arneil Walker 1986
CLACKMANNAN AND THE OCHILS by Adam Swan 1987
THE DISTRICT OF MORAY by Charles McKean 1987
CENTRAL GLASGOW by Charles McKean, David Walker and Frank A Walker reprint 1993
BANFF & BUCHAN by Charles McKean 1990
SHETLAND by Mike Finnie 1990
THE KINGDOM OF FIFE by Glen Pride 1990
ORKNEY by Leslie Burgher 1991
ROSS & CROMARTY by Elizabeth Beaton 1992
THE MONKLANDS by Allan Peden 1992
THE NORTH CLYDE ESTUARY by Frank Arneil Walker and Fiona Sinclair 1992
AYRSHIRE & ARRAN by Rob Close 1992
WEST LOTHIAN by Richard Jaques and Charles McKean 1994
BORDERS & BERWICK by Charles A Strang 1994
GORDON by Ian Shepherd 1994
SUTHERLAND by Elizabeth Beaton 1995

— *Forthcoming* —

CENTRAL LOWLANDS by Richard Jaques and Allan Peden
DUMFRIES & GALLOWAY by John Hume and Judith Anderson

ARE YOU BUILDING UP THE SET?

The RIAS/Landmark Trust series is winner of the *Glenfiddich Living Scotland Award 1985*
These and other RIAS books and books on world architecture are all available from RIAS
Bookshops at 15 Rutland Square, Edinburgh EH1 2BE, Tel 0131-229 7545
and 545 Sauchiehall Street, Glasgow G3 7PQ, Tel 0141-221 6496